Turks and Caicos Travel Guide 2023-2024

Discover the Ultimate Destination for relaxation and Adventure. Everything you need to know Before Planning a Trip to Turks and Caicos

GENEVA WALKER

CONTENTS

INTRODUCTION
About Turks and Caicos

Welcome to Turks and Caicos, an overseas territory of the British Empire made consisting of two clusters of tropical islands in the northern West Indies and the Atlantic Ocean. They are largely known as an offshore financial centre and for tourism center, but they have so much more to offer: stunning natural beauty, rich culture and history, diverse and abundant wildlife, exciting activities and adventures, delicious food and drinks, friendly and hospitable people, and a relaxed and laid-back vibe.

Turks and Caicos is a location that will appeal to all types of tourists, whether you are looking for a love break, a family holiday, a single journey, or a group trip with friends. You can choose from various housing choices, from luxury resorts and homes to cozy guesthouses and cottages. You can also explore the different islands and cays that make up the group, each with charm and character.

Turks and Caicos is a location where you may experience the finest of both worlds, relax and unwind on some of the world's most beautiful beaches, such as Grace Bay Beach, which is considered to be among the greatest beaches in the world; or you can get active and adventurous on land or water, such as scuba diving among coral reefs and shipwrecks, whale watching in Salt Cay, hiking in Middle Caicos, or kite surfing in Long Bay Beach.

Turks and Caicos is also a place where you can learn and discover: you can immerse yourself in the culture and history of the islands, such as visiting the National Museum in Grand Turk, where you can see exhibits on the pre-Columbian inhabitants, the European colonization, the slave trade, the salt industry, the space program and more; or you can experience the nature and wildlife of the islands, such as visiting little Water Cay to witness the threatened rock iguanas; or Pine Cay, where you can snorkel among colorful fish.

Turks and Caicos is a place that will surprise and delight you: you will find hidden gems and secrets that will make your trip unforgettable, such as ancient carvings on the rocks in Sapodilla Bay Beach; celebrity villas in Parrot Cay; flamingo ponds in North Caicos; or local delicacies such as conch fritters, peas and rice, or rum cake.

Turks and Caicos is a place that will inspire you:

- You will meet amazing people sharing their stories and tips with you.
- You will see breathtaking sights that make you want to capture them with your camera.
- You will experience fun activities that will make you feel alive.
- You will taste delicious food.
- You will drink refreshing drinks that will quench your thirst.
- You will relax and enjoy every moment.

Turks and Caicos is a place you will love: it is beautiful by nature and people, it is a place that you will always enjoy and you will want to visit again soon.

This trip plan for 2023-2024 is gathered by locals who have visited widely in Turks and Caicos. It includes all the information, tips, advice and secrets needed to plan your trip, make choices on the road, and experience Turks and Caicos in a great way. It is an amazing guide to Turks and Caicos, and we hope you will find it useful and fun.

Visitation Story

Turks and Caicos Islands has always been on my bucket list, a British Overseas Territory made of two groups of tropical islands in the Atlantic Ocean and northern West Indies. They are known mainly for tourists and as a foreign financial center, but I was more interested in their natural beauty, culture and history.

I planned my trip to Turks and Caicos for a year, studying the best time to go, the best places to stay, the best things to do and the best ways to get around. I chose to go in June when it was a warm, bright day and not very hot or muggy. I booked a flight to Providenciales, the largest Island and entrance to the rest of the group. I also booked a hotel on Grace Bay Beach, ranked as one of the best beaches in the world.

I was stunned by the beauty of Turks and Caicos when I arrived. The blue seas, the white sand beaches, the palm trees and the gentle breeze were all inviting me to rest and enjoy. I checked in to my hotel and was met by friendly staff who offered me a welcome drink and a map of the Island. I unpacked my bags and went to the beach right away, where

I spent the remainder of the day swimming, sunbathing and reading.

The next day, I chose to explore more of Providenciales. I got a car and went around the Island, stopping at different places of interest. I went to Chalk Sound National Park, where I saw a beautiful lake with hundreds of tiny islands. I also visited Sapodilla Bay Beach, where I saw old drawings on the rocks left by lost sailors. I also went to Blue Hills, where I learned about the salt business that was once the islands' primary source of revenue.

On my third day, I wanted to see other islands and cays that make up Turks and Caicos. I booked a boat tour that took me to several of them, including Little Water Cay, where I saw endangered rock iguanas; Pine Cay, where I snorkeled among colorful coral reefs; Parrot Cay, where I saw celebrities' villas; and North Caicos, where I visited Flamingo Pond Nature Reserve and saw hundreds of pink flamingos.

On my fourth day, I had an amazing experience I will never forget. I went whale watching with a local guide who took me to Salt Cay, a small island south of Grand Turk. I watched one of nature's most amazing shows: humpback whales moving from their food grounds in the North Atlantic to their breeding grounds in the Caribbean. I saw them breaking, spitting, tail-slapping and singing. It was awe-inspiring and humbling at the same time.

On my fifth day, I chose to go scuba diving with a reputable dive company that took me to some of the best dive spots in Turks and Caicos. I was blown away by the variety and wealth of marine life I saw: sharks, rays, turtles, dolphins, lobsters, crabs, octopuses and endless fish types. I also explored some ships that dot the ocean floor, such as the H.M.S. Endymion, a British warship that sank in 1790 during a fight with a French ship.

On my sixth day, I wanted to learn more about the society and past of Turks and Caicos. I went to Grand Turk, the city and ancient center of the region. There, I toured the National Museum, where I learned about the pre-Columbian people of the islands, the European settlement, the slave trade, the salt business, the space program and more. I also went to Cockburn Town, where British houses returned to the 18th century.

On my seventh day, I relaxed and enjoyed my last day on Grace Bay Beach. I met some amazing people who became friends during my stay: locals who shared their stories and tips with me; fellow travelers who exchanged experiences and recommendations with me; hotel staff who treated me like family; tour guides who showed me around with passion and enthusiasm; dive instructors who taught me new skills and techniques; boat captains who made me laugh and feel safe; shop owners who offered me souvenirs and gifts; restaurant owners who served me delicious food and drinks; spa therapists who pampered me with massages and treatments; musicians who entertained me with live music; artists who inspired me with their creations; and many more.

I had a great time during my stay in Turks and Caicos. I explored the beautiful islands and cays, and I met wonderful people. I learned new things, saw amazing sights, did exciting activities, ate delicious food, drank refreshing drinks, relaxed and enjoyed. I also prepared a travel guide for 2023/2024 with useful information from experts that will help tourists experience Turks and Caicos in a great way. It contains all the information, tips, advice and secrets I found during my trip. It is the best guide to Turks and Caicos, and I hope you will find it useful and fun.

Turks and Caicos is a location that I will always remember. It is beautiful by nature and filled with amazing people. It is a place I will always treasure and hope to visit again soon.

History of Turks and Caicos

Turks and Caicos have a rich and interesting history covering ages and countries. From the pre-Columbian people to the European conquerors, from the pirates and buccaneers to the loyalists and farmers, from the salt rakers to the space pioneers, the islands have watched many events and changes that have shaped their identity and fate.

The Lucayans and Tainos

The first known settlers of Turks and Caicos were the Lucayans and Tainos, two groups of Arawakan-speaking people who moved from Hispaniola and Cuba around 700 AD. They settled mainly in Middle Caicos and Grand Turk, where they created a peaceful and prosperous society based on farming, fishing, trade and crafting.

They grew crops such as corn, beans, cassava, sweet potatoes and cotton; they fished conch, crab, turtle and fish; they traded salt, dried conch, beads and pottery with other islands; they made boats, baskets, hammocks, jewelry and tools. They also had a complex spiritual system that involved events, rites, dances and songs.

The Lucayans and Tainos lived in peace with nature and each other for almost 800 years until the coming of the Europeans in the late 15th century. The first recorded sighting of Turks and Caicos by a European was by Christopher Columbus in 1492, who may have landed on Grand Turk during his first journey to the New World.

However, some historians think that Juan Ponce de Leon first visited the islands in 1512 during his search for the Fountain of Youth. In either case, the touch with the Europeans proved disastrous for the Lucayans and Tainos, who were soon kidnapped, abused, sick and destroyed by the Spanish invaders. By 1520, the islands were virtually depopulated and abandoned.

Columbus and Early Explorers

The discovery of Turks and Caicos by Columbus sparked a wave of exploration and settlement by European forces in the Caribbean. The islands were claimed by Spain, France, England and Holland at different times, but they all needed to build stable villages or forts. The islands were generally used as a salt source, an important product for keeping food in those days. The Spanish were the first to mine the natural salt ponds on Grand Turk and Salt Cay, where they put the Lucayans to work as salt rakers. The French also tried to develop a salt business in South Caicos in the 17th century, but the English drove them away.

The English were the most dogged in their attempts to settle Turks and Caicos. They first claimed the islands in 1625 under King James I but did not send any residents until 1678 under King Charles II. They gave a charter to Bermudian salt traders who started a yearly salt trade on Grand Turk and Salt Cay. They also built a small fort on Grand Turk to protect their interests from pirates and enemy countries. The English also claimed authority over the Caicos Islands in 1706 under Queen Anne, but they settled them later.

Pirates and Buccaneers

The 17th and 18th centuries were the pinnacle of the golden period of pirates in the Caribbean. Many pirates and buccaneers roamed the seas in search of plunder and excitement. Some of them occasionally used Turks and Caicos as a base or hideout. The islands gave them protected ports, fresh water, food supplies, salt for drying meat, wood for fixing ships, wealth for hiding or recovering, and enslaved people for selling or hiring.

Some of the most prominent pirates who visited Turks and Caicos were Anne Bonny, Mary Read, Calico Jack Rackham, Blackbeard (Edward Teach), Stede Bonnet, Henry Morgan and François l'Olonnais. They attacked Spanish ships loaded with gold and silver from Mexico and Peru; they raided French farms on Hispaniola and Tortuga; they fought against English warships and privateers; they partnered with or betrayed each other; they lived by their code of honor and cruelty.

The pirate age came to an end in the early 18th century when the European powers cracked down on piracy and offered pardons or prizes for those who submitted or turned informers. Some pirates took forgiveness and became legal traders or farmers; some continued their outlaw life until they were caught or killed; some moved to remote islands or mainland colonies; and some disappeared into legend and mystery.

The Salt Industry

The salt business was the major economic activity and the lifeline of Turks and Caicos for over 300 years. It began in the late 16th century when the Spanish and the French started to collect salt from the natural salt ponds on Grand Turk and Salt Cay. It continued in the 17th and 18th centuries when the English and the Bermudians started a yearly salt trade on the same islands. It peaked in the 19th century, when the Turks Islands became one of the biggest salt producers in the world, providing markets in North America, Europe and Africa.

The salt business was based on a simple but laborious process:

The seawater was directed into small ponds, melting under the sun and leaving behind a layer of salt crystals. The salt was then raked, piled, dried, bagged and shipped to the docks, where it was put onto sailing boats and carried to foreign places.

The salt business hired hundreds of workers, mostly enslaved people and later freedmen, who suffered hard conditions and low pay. The salt business also drew traders, farmers, shipowners, leaders, sailors, agents and officials, who made or lost riches in the chaotic salt market.

The salt industry declined in the late 19th and early 20th centuries due to several factors:

Competition from other salt producers, such as Haiti and Venezuela Changes in consumer preferences, such as refined salt and refrigeration Natural disasters, such as hurricanes and floods Social unrest, such as slave revolts and labor strikes Political instability, such as wars and revolutions Technological innovations, such as steamships and railways

The last salt export from Turks and Caicos occurred in 1964, marking the end of an age.

Loyalists and Plantations

The American Revolution (1775-1783) had a major effect on Turks and Caicos. Many supporters, or colonists loyal to Britain during the war, ran from their homes in the American colonies and found shelter in other British areas, such as the Bahamas, Jamaica and Turks and Caicos. They brought with them their families, enslaved people, animals, furniture and goods. They also brought their skills, knowledge, cash and desire.

Some supporters moved to Grand Turk and Salt Cay, where they worked in the salt trade or other companies. Some of them moved to Providenciales, where they created a sponge industry or a fishing business. But most of them moved to the Caicos Islands, where they created cotton farms on big areas of land given by the British Crown.

The loyalists hoped to recreate their former wealth and lifestyle in their new home. They built beautiful homes, parks, churches, schools and mills. They grew cotton, indigo, sisal and food. They traded with other places and countries. They formed a society based on class, race and faith.

However, their dreams soon turned into fears. The cotton farms proved to be unprofitable and unstable. The land was poor and barren. The temperature was hot and dry. The bugs were numerous and damaging. The markets were uncertain and fierce. The slaves were unruly and resistant. The supporters were separated and exposed.

By the early 19th century, most of the supporters had abandoned their farms and left Turks and Caicos. Some returned to Britain or America. Some moved to other Caribbean islands. Some died of disease or murder. Only a few stayed and adapted to their new conditions.

The followers left behind a heritage of ruins, relics and papers that tell their story. They also left behind a tradition of black and white offspring, who received their genes, names and culture.

The Victorian and Industrial Era

The 19th century was a time of change and development for Turks and Caicos. Political changes, social movements, economic difficulties, cultural impacts, and technical advances marked it.

Politically, Turks and Caicos suffered several changes in their position and government within the British Empire. In 1799, it became part of the Bahamas. In 1848, it became part of Jamaica. In 1874, it became a separate colony under a commissioner. In 1876-1877, it was briefly seized by

Canada. From 1917-1962, it was again part of Jamaica. From 1962-1973, it was part of the Bahamas again. In 1973-present, it became a British Overseas Territory with its ruler.

Socially, Turks and Caicos watched several trends that changed its people and society. In 1807-1833, slavery was ended throughout the British Empire, saving thousands of enslaved people in Turks and Caicos.

In 1834-1840, a training system was adopted to replace slavery, but it was also ended due to its abuses and errors. In 1841-1861, a contract labor system was adopted to control the labor market, but it was also attacked for its abuse and discrimination. In 1862-1900, a system of immigration was created to draw workers from other islands and countries, such as Haiti, Dominican Republic, Jamaica, Bermuda and Turks Islands. These moves resulted in a varied and lively society that reflected different races, cultures, languages and faiths.

Economically, Turks and Caicos faced several problems that affected its growth and wealth. The fall of the salt business in the late 19th century left the islands with few sources of income and jobs. The rise of the sponge business in the early 20th century brought some hope and chance, but it was also short-lived due to overfishing and disease. The rise of the tourism business in the mid-20th century offered a new and bright field, but it was also based on external forces such as demand, supply, competition and control. These problems pushed the islands to seek help and support from Britain and other countries.

Culturally, Turks and Caicos faced several factors that changed its character and expression. The British impact was obvious in the law system, the school system, the government system and the language. The American impact was obvious in the media, the pleasure, the shopping and the lifestyle. The Caribbean impact was obvious in the music, the food, the art and the culture. These factors produced a unique and mixed society that combined custom and technology.

Technologically, Turks and Caicos experienced several advances that affected its connection and transportation. The development of the telegraph in the mid-19th century allowed faster and easier touch with other islands and countries. The invention of the steamboat in the late 19th century allowed better and cheaper travel by sea. The creation of the airplane in the early 20th century allowed faster and more comfortable journeys by air. The creation of the radio in the mid-20th century allowed wider and more diverse access to information and pleasure. These innovations opened up new frontiers and opportunities for Turks and Caicos.

The history of Turks and Caicos is a tale of change and adaptability. The islands have seen many people come and go, many events happen and pass, many challenges appear and overcome, many factors shape and remake, and many ideas create and rebuild. The islands have also kept and maintained their character and beauty, history and legacy, values and beliefs, customs and practices, and dreams and ambitions.

The history of Turks and Caicos is also a tale of finding and travel. Different people have found and studied the islands at different times for different reasons and goals. The islands have also asked and accepted tourists to find and explore them, to learn and appreciate them, to enjoy and respect them, and to love and protect them.

Geography

The Turks and Caicos Islands are a British Overseas Territory in the Caribbean, made of two groups of islands: the Turks Islands and the Caicos Islands. They are situated on the southeastern edge of the Bahamas group, north of Hispaniola, about 1,000 km (620 mi) from Miami, U.S.A. The islands have a total land area of 430 sq km (170 sq mi) and a population of about 57,000 people.

Turks Islands

The Turks Islands are the smaller and easternmost group of islands, containing Grand Turk, Salt Cay, and several smaller cays and rocks. Grand Turk is the region's capital and major economic center, as well as the political and cultural hub. It has a land size of 18 sq km (7 sq mi) and a population of about 5,600 people. Salt Cay is the second biggest Island in the group, with a land area of 6.7 sq km (2.6 sq mi) and a population of about 100 people. The Turks Islands are named after the Turk's head cactus, a local plant that resembles a fez.

28

The Turks Islands are low-lying and flat, with an average slope of less than 10 m (33 ft). They are made of limestone and coral rocks and have numerous salt ponds and lakes. The islands have a dry and sunny climate, with an average yearly rainfall of less than 600 mm (24 in). The islands are surrounded by beautiful blue seas and coral reefs, which draw many tourists for diving, swimming, fishing, and whale watching. The Turks Island Passage, or "the Wall," is a deep ocean trench that divides the Turks Islands from the Caicos Islands, reaching depths of over 2,000 m (6,600 ft).

Caicos Islands

The Caicos Islands are the bigger and westernmost group of islands, containing six main islands: South Caicos, East Caicos, Middle Caicos, North Caicos, Providenciales, and West Caicos, and several smaller cays and flats. Providenciales is the group's most popular and developed Island, with a land area of 98 sq km (38 sq mi) and a population of about 36,000 people. It is home to the international airport, upscale villas, golf fields, shopping areas, and piers. South Caicos is the second biggest Island in the group, with a land area of 21 sq km (8 sq mi) and a population of about 1,500 people. It is the fishing capital of the region, with a natural dock, a fish processing plant, and a marine study station. The other islands in the group are less crowded and more rural, with lush greenery, caves, marshes, hills, and beaches. The Caicos Islands are taken from the Lucayan word "caya hico," meaning "string of islands."

The Caicos Islands are slightly higher and hillier than the Turks Islands, with an average elevation of about 15 m (49 ft) and a highest point of 48 m (157 ft) on Providenciales. They are also made of limestone and coral rocks but have richer land and watery sources. The islands have a tropical grassland climate, with an average yearly rainfall of about 1,000 mm (40 in), mostly in summer. The islands are also ringed by beautiful blue seas and coral reefs, which form part of the third-largest barrier reef system in the world. The Caicos Bank is a flat bank that covers most of the area between the islands, reaching depths of less than 10 m (33 ft). It is rich in marine life and aragonite sand layers.

CHAPTER 1
PLANNING YOUR TRIP TO TURKS AND CAICOS

Turks and Caicos is a dream location for many tourists, with its gorgeous blue waves, white-sand beaches, coral reefs, and laid-back vibe. Whether you're looking for a romantic trip, a family holiday, or an adventure-filled escape, you'll find plenty of choices to fit your tastes and budget.

The Island is a beautiful location that offers tourists a mix of history, culture, and technology, with its beautiful islands, stunning buildings, and rich cultural history. Turks and Caicos is a place for visitors and tourists who are looking for a perfect, unique and great experience.

In this chapter, we will provide you with tips and advice on how to plan your trip to Turks and Caicos. From choosing the best time to visit to finding the best places to stay and the top sites to see. we will cover all the important information you need to make your trip successful.

Whether you are a solo tourist or planning a family vacation, read on as we reveal how to plan your dream trip to Tucks and Caicos.

When to go to Turks and Caicos

Turks and Caicos is year-round with warm and sunny weather, beautiful beaches, and stunning coral reefs. However, based on your interests and goals, some months may be better than others to visit this Caribbean paradise. Here are some things to consider when picking the best time to visit Turk's and Caicos.

Weather

The weather in Turks and Caicos is usually nice and constant throughout the year, with average highs running from 27°C (81°F) in January to 32°C (90°F) in July. The islands have a warm climate, with two main seasons: the dry season from December to April and the wet season from May to November. The dry season is cooler, drier, and less humid than the wet season, which is hotter, wetter, and more humid. The wet season also overlaps with the storm season, which runs from June to November.

Although big storms are rare in Turks and Caicos, they can still pose a threat and disrupt trip plans. The islands are also prone to rare tropical storms and rains, especially from August to October.

The best time to visit Turks and Caicos for good weather is from April to May when the temperatures are warm but not too hot, the rainfall is low but not too dry, and the humidity is normal but not too high. This is also a sweet spot between the peak and rainy seasons when the islands are less busy and cheaper.

Crowds

The peak season in Turks and Caicos goes from December to April, when the islands attract the most tourists, especially from North America and Europe. This is also the time when most cruise ships stop at Grand Turk, bringing thousands of tourists every day. The peak season overlaps with the winter holidays, spring break, and Easter, when many tourists seek a warm escape from the cold weather. During this time, the islands are busy with activities but also more expensive and crowded. You may need to book your flights, hotels, and activities well in advance and expect higher rates and longer queues.

The off-season in Turks and Caicos runs from May to November, when the islands receive fewer tourists, especially from June to October. This is also when some hotels and restaurants close down or undergo repairs. During this time, the islands are quieter and cheaper but more prone to rain and storms. You may find more access and freedom to visit the islands at your own pace, but also less variety and choices for eating and activities.

The holiday season in Turks and Caicos runs from late April to early May and from late November to early December when the weather is nice, the prices are reasonable, and the crowds are thinner. This is an ideal time to visit if you want to escape the extremes of both seasons and enjoy the best of both worlds.

Events

Turks and Caicos hosts several events and fairs annually, celebrating its culture, music, food, sports, and nature. Some of the most famous shows include:

- **Junkanoo Jump Up:** A street show on Boxing Day (December 26) and New Year's Day (January 1), featuring bright outfits, music, dancing, food, and drinks.

- **Turks & Caicos Music & Cultural event:** A week-long event that takes place in late July or early August on Providenciales, featuring local and foreign acts playing different styles of music.

- **Conch event:** A food event that takes place in late November on Providenciales, featuring conch meals made by local cooks, as well as live music, arts, crafts, and games.

- **Whale Watching Season:** A natural event from January to April, when humpback whales pass through the Turks Island Passage and can be seen from the beach or on boat tours.

- **Kite Flying Competition:** A family-friendly event that takes place on Easter Monday on Grand Turk, featuring kite flying games, awards, food, and fun.

Turks and Caicos is a wonderful place to visit any time of the year, but some months may offer more benefits than others based on your tastes and goals. Whether looking for good weather, smaller people, cheap prices, or exciting events, you'll find something to fit your taste and budget in this Caribbean paradise. No matter where you go, you'll be amazed by the beauty and charm of the islands and their people.

How to get to Turks and Caicos

Turks and Caicos is a British Overseas Territory made of two groups of tropical islands in the Atlantic Ocean and northern West Indies. It is about 575 miles (925 km) southeast of Miami, Florida, and 39 miles (63 km) south of the Bahamas. It has a total land size of 193 square miles (500 square km) and a population of about 38,000.

There are two main ways to get to Turks and Caicos: by plane or by cruise ship. Depending on your location, income, taste and schedule, you can choose the option that suits you best. Here are some tips and information to help you plan your trip.

By Plane

The most popular and easiest way to get to Turk's and Caicos is by plane. Many planes are available in the United States, Canada, the United Kingdom, the Caribbean and other countries. You can also find holidays or special trips from other locations.

The largest airport in Turks and Caicos is the Providenciales International Airport (P.L.S.), situated on the Island of

Providenciales (Provo), the country's most developed and crowded Island. It is also the entrance to the rest of the islands, as you can take local planes or boats from there.

To visit Turks and Caicos by plane, you need a current visa and a return or onward ticket. You may also need a visa based on your country. See Passports and Visas for more information. You will also need to fill out a visa and customs statement forms upon arriving. You may be asked to show proof of lodging and sufficient funds for your stay.

There are limits on the amounts and kinds of things you can bring into Turks and Caicos duty-free. See Customs Allowances for more information. If you are going with pets, you will need a medical license and an import permit. See Traveling with Pets for more information.

Once you clear immigration and customs, you can take a taxi or rent a car to get to your hotel. There is no public transportation or bus service on the Island. See Getting Around for more information.

Here are some of the airlines that fly to Turks and Caicos:

- American Airlines: from Miami, Charlotte, Philadelphia, New York (J.F.K.), Boston, Chicago (O'Hare) and Dallas (Fort Worth).
- Delta Air Lines: from Atlanta, New York (J.F.K.) and Boston.
- JetBlue Airways: from New York (J.F.K.), Boston, Fort Lauderdale and Newark.
- United Airlines: from Newark, Houston (Intercontinental) and Chicago (O'Hare).
- Southwest Airlines: from Baltimore, Fort Lauderdale and Houston (Hobby).
- Air Canada: from Toronto, Montreal and Ottawa.
- WestJet: from Toronto.
- British Airways: from London (Gatwick) via Antigua.
- InterCaribbean Airways: from Antigua, Bahamas (Nassau), Cuba (Havana), Dominican Republic (Santo Domingo), Haiti (Port-au-Prince), Jamaica (Kingston) and Puerto Rico (San Juan).
- Caicos Express Airways: from Bahamas (Nassau) and Dominican Republic (Santiago).
- Bahamasair: from Bahamas (Nassau).

By Cruise Ship

Another way to get to Turks and Caicos is by cruise ship. Many ship lines stop at Grand Turk, the country's city and historical center. A modern ship center offers shops, restaurants, bars, pools, beaches, trips and entertainment.

To visit Turks and Caicos by cruise ship, you do not need a passport or visa if you are a citizen or legal resident of the United States, Canada or the United Kingdom. However, we suggest that you take a legal visa anyway in case of accidents or changes in plans. You will also need to fill out an immigration form given by your ship line.

There are no limits on the amounts or kinds of things you can bring into Turks and Caicos duty-free as long as they are for personal use only. However, there may be limits on what you can bring back to your home country. Check with your ship line or customs officials for more information.

Once you exit your cruise ship, you can explore Grand Turk on foot or by cab. There are many sights and activities to enjoy on the Island, such as visiting the National Museum, walking Cockburn Town, swimming at Gibbs Cay, riding horses on the beach or riding sand cars on the salt flats. See Things to Do for more information.

Here are some of the cruise lines that stop at Grand Turk:

- Carnival Cruise Line
- Holland America Line
- Norwegian Cruise Line
- Princess Cruises
- Royal Caribbean International
- Celebrity Cruises
- Disney Cruise Line
- M.S.C. Cruises
- Oceania Cruises
- Regent Seven Seas Cruises
- Seabourn Cruise Line
- Silversea Cruises

By Yacht

Another way to get to Turks and Caicos is by boat. Many yachters and tourists visit the islands to enjoy the clean seas, the beautiful cays, the abundant marine life and the friendly harbors. Turks and Caicos have several ports of entry where you can clear customs and immigration and many anchorages and sites where you can stay.

You need a legal visa and a return or onward ticket to enter Turks and Caicos by boat. You may also need a visa based on your country. See Passports and Visas for more information. You will also need to fill out a visa and customs statement forms upon arriving. You may be asked to show proof of insurance, registration, ownership and safety devices.

There are limits on the amounts and kinds of things you can bring into Turks and Caicos duty-free. See Customs Allowances for more information. If you are going with pets, you will need a medical license and an import permit. See Traveling with Pets for more information.

You will also need to pay a cruise fee based on the size and length of your vehicle. The fee goes from $50 to $300 for up to seven days or from $150 to $900 for up to 90 days. You can pay the fee at any port of entry or online at www.tcimarineandports.com.

Here are some of the ports of entry in Turks and Caicos:

- Providenciales: Blue Haven Marina, Turtle Cove Marina, South Side Marina.
- Grand Turk: Grand Turk Cruise Center, Cockburn Town Harbour.
- Salt Cay: Deane's Dock.
- South Caicos: South Caicos Marina.
- North Caicos: Sandy Point Marina.

Here are some of the anchorages and piers in Turks and Caicos:

- Providenciales: Sapodilla Bay, Chalk Sound, Grace Bay, Leeward Cut, Long Bay.
- Grand Turk: Governor's Beach, White Sands Beach, Pillory Beach.
- Salt Cay: Balfour Town Harbour, North Beach.
- South Caicos: Cockburn Harbour, Bell Sound, Long Cay.
- North Caicos: Bottle Creek Lagoon, Whitby Beach, Horsestable Beach.
- Middle Caicos: Bambarra Beach, Mudjin Harbour, Conch Bar.

- East Caicos: Jacksonville Beach, Wild Cow Run.
- West Caicos: West Caicos Marine National Park.

Turks and Caicos is an easy and handy location to get to by plane or cruise ship. You can also get to the islands by boat if you have your vessel or hire one. Depending on your way of transportation, you will need to follow certain standards and processes to enter the country officially and easily. You must also plan your onward journey to your hotel or other islands.

Getting Around Turks and Caicos

Turks and Caicos is a stunning collection of nine settled islands and many smaller cays and islands, each with charm and attractions. Whether you want to discover the colorful coral reefs, the historic towns, the clean beaches or the nature parks, you'll need to know how to get around this tropical paradise.

By Air

The main entrance to Turks and Caicos is the Providenciales International Airport (P.L.S.), which gets flights from many big places in North America and Europe and other Caribbean islands. From there, you can catch local trips to Grand Turk, South Caicos and Salt Cay, run by interCaribbean and Caicos Express. These flights are short (15 to 30 minutes) and offer amazing views of the blue seas and the cays below. You can also charter trips to North Caicos, which has a small airport but no regular service.

By Sea

Another way to move between the islands is by passenger boat, which can be a beautiful and relaxing choice. There are three boat lines in Turks and Caicos: Providenciales-

North Caicos, Providenciales-South Caicos and Grand Turk-Salt Cay. The Providenciales-North Caicos boat is the most regular, with multiple daily runs. It takes about 30 minutes and costs $25 one way or $50 round trip. The Providenciales-South Caicos boat runs several times per week, takes about 90 minutes and costs $50 one way or $90 round trip. The Grand Turk-Salt Cay boat runs twice per week, takes about 30 minutes and costs $15 one way or $25 round trip. You can buy tickets online or at the boat ports.

By Car

Renting a car is a great way to explore the islands at your own pace and ease. You can find car rental companies at the airport, the cruise center, and key towns. Rates range based on the type of vehicle and the season but plan to pay around $60 to $80 per day for a cheap car or a truck. You'll need a legal driver's license from your home country and a foreign driving pass if your license needs to be English. You'll also need to pay a $15 temporary driver's license fee.

Driving in Turks and Caicos is on the left side of the road, as in the U.K. Most roads have a speed limit of 20 mph (32 km/h), but some cars may go faster. Be careful of potholes, walkers, bikers and animals on the road. Most roads are paved, but some are dirt or clay. Gas stations are available on all occupied islands but may close early or run out of fuel.

By Taxi

Taxis are another choice for getting around Turks and Caicos, especially if you want to avoid driving or renting a car. You can find cabs at the airport, the shipping center, and big towns. You can call them or ask your hotel to plan one for you. Taxis are paid or have set fares based on the location. Rates are per person and each way. For example, from the shipping center to Governor's Beach, it's $4; to Cockburn Town, it's $5; and to the Grand Turk Lighthouse, it's $9. Make sure to check the fare before you get in.

By Bike or Scooter

If you're feeling brave, you can take a bike or a scooter to explore the islands on two wheels. This can be a fun and eco-friendly way to see the sights, especially on smaller islands like Grand Turk or Salt Cay. You can take bikes or scooters at some hotels, spas or hire companies. Rates are around $20 to $25 per day for a bike and $75 for a scooter.

You'll need a helmet, a lock and sunscreen. Be aware of driving rules and road conditions.

By Foot

Walking is not a realistic way to get around Turks and Caicos, as the sights, shops and hotels are spread out over big areas. However, walking can be fun for short distances or for visiting specific places, such as old Cockburn Town on Grand Turk or Grace Bay Beach on Providenciales. Just remember to wear comfy shoes, a hat and sunscreen.

Turks and Caicos is a beautiful location that gives something to everyone. Whether you fly, sail, drive, ride or walk, you'll find amazing places and events that will make your trip memorable.

Turks and Caicos is a stunning collection of nine settled islands and many smaller cays and islands, each with charm and attractions. Whether you want to discover the colorful coral reefs, the historic towns, the clean beaches or the nature parks, you'll need to know how to get around this tropical paradise.

Tips and Advice

- Book your flights, boats and car hires in advance, especially during peak season or holidays, as they may sell out or increase in price.

- Check the weather report before your journey, as it may change your plans. Hurricanes are likely from June to November and may cause flying or boat delays or cancellations.

- Carry cash with you, as some places may not accept credit cards or charge extra fees. The legal currency is the U.S. dollar, but some places may accept other currencies at a lower exchange rate.

- Respect the local culture and practices, and dress properly. Turks and Caicos is a British Overseas Territory with a strict religious culture. Avoid wearing exposed or inappropriate clothes, especially in public places or holy sites.

- Protect yourself from the sun, heat and animals. Wear sunscreen, sunglasses, a hat and light clothes.

Drink plenty of water and avoid alcohol or coffee. Use bug protection and cover up when mosquitoes are most busy at dusk and dawn.

- Be safe and responsible when driving, walking or scooting. Follow the road rules, wear a seat belt or a helmet, and don't drink and drive. Avoid driving at night or on unknown roads. Lock your car, and don't leave belongings inside.

- Be eco-friendly and respectful of the earth. Don't litter, trash or energy, or harm wildlife. Follow the rules and laws of the national parks and sea areas. Don't touch, feed or harass the animals, especially the rare ones. Don't gather shells, reefs or plants.

Choosing the right Accommodations

Turks and Caicos is a stunning collection of 40 islands and cays, each with its own charm and character. Whether you're looking for a romantic break, a family-friendly adventure, or a relaxing vacation, you'll find various options to fit your needs and price.

Types of Accommodations

You can choose from different types of hotels in Turks and Caicos, such as:

Resorts: These are big and full-service buildings that offer features like pools, spas, restaurants, bars, activities, and entertainment. Resorts are ideal for those who want to enjoy everything in one place and are okay with paying extra for ease and comfort. Most resorts are on Providenciales, the main Island, especially along the popular Grace Bay Beach. Some examples of places are Seven Stars Resort & Spa, Point Grace, and The Shore Club.

All-inclusive resorts: These are resorts that include eating, on-site events, and other perks with room rates. All-inclusive vacations are great for those who want to relax and not worry about planning or spending on food and activities. However, they can also be more expensive and restrictive than other choices and may offer little range or local culture. There are nine all-inclusive resorts in Turks and Caicos, five on Providenciales and four on other islands. Some examples of all-inclusive resorts are Beaches Turks & Caicos, Club Med Turkoise, and Amanyara.

Hotels: These are smaller and easier places that offer basic facilities like rooms, showers, air conditioning, and Wi-Fi. Hotels are great for those who want to save money and have more freedom and independence. Hotels can be found on most islands, but they tend to be more basic and rural on the less-developed ones. Some examples of hotels are The Oasis at Grace Bay, Le Vele Resort, and Osprey Beach Hotel.

Villas: These self-catering homes offer more room, privacy, and comfort than hotels or motels. Villas are ideal for those who want to feel at home and have more control over their stay. Villas can range from flats to beach houses and suit different group sizes and tastes. Villas can be rented through online sites or local agents. Some examples of houses are Villa Renaissance, Coral Gardens on Grace Bay, and The Meridian Club.

Factors to Consider

When picking your hotel in Turks and Caicos, you should consider the following factors:

Location: Turks and Caicos have many islands, but most tourist equipment centers on Providenciales. If you want to explore other islands, you'll need to take buses or boat tours, which can add time and cost to your trip. You should also consider the closeness of your hotel to the beach, the airport, the shops, the restaurants, and the sites that interest you.

Budget: Turks and Caicos is a costly location, so you should plan your budget carefully and check prices before booking. Generally speaking, resorts and all-inclusive resorts are more expensive than hotels and houses, but they may also offer more value for money based on what's included. You should also add the taxes, fees, tips, transportation, food, and exercise costs that may apply to your stay.

Style: Turks and Caicos has various hotels catering to different styles and personalities. You can find chic and modern properties that offer luxury and style, cozy and charming properties that offer warmth and character, or simple and rural properties that offer authenticity and peace. You should choose a hotel that fits your style and mood.

Services: Turks and Caicos has a range of services that can improve your stay and make it more relaxing and fun. Before booking, you should check what services your accommodation offers, such as Wi-Fi, air conditioning, T.V., kitchen facilities, laundry facilities, pool access, spa access, gym access, restaurant access, bar access, activity access, butler service, room service, cleaning service, etc.

Summary

Turks and Caicos is a beautiful location that offers a wide selection of lodging for every visitor. You can choose from resorts, all-inclusive resorts, hotels, or houses, based on your wants and interests. You should consider your hotel's location, price, style, services, and reviews before booking.

Whatever you choose, you'll be sure to have an amazing stay in Turks and Caicos.

What to pack

Packing for Turks and Caicos can be a breeze if you follow some easy rules and tips. The islands have a warm environment, so you'll need light, casual, and comfy clothes and items for most activities. You'll also need some basics to protect yourself from the sun, the insects, and the odd rain shower. Here are some ideas on what to pack for your Turks and Caicos trip.

Clothing

- **Shorts:** Bring a few pairs for touring, boating, playing tennis, or just sitting around. Opt for light-colored shorts and fabrics to keep you cool and comfy.

- **T-shirts:** Pack some in different colors and styles to match your shorts. You can also wear them as cover-ups over your swimsuits.

- **Swimsuits:** You'll need at least two swimsuits for your trip, as you'll spend much time in the water.

Choose outfits that fit well and flatter your figure. You can also bring a rash guard or a wetsuit if you plan to do swimming or diving.

- **Dresses and skirts:** For women, dresses and skirts are flexible and easy to pack. Wear them for casual trips, beach days, or dinner dates. Choose dresses and skirts in light fabrics, bright colors, and fun prints.

- **Shirts:** For guys, shirts are useful for cooler nights, formal events, or trips to religious places. Choose pants and shirts in light fabrics, basic colors, and classic styles.

- **Shoes:** You'll need a few kinds of shoes for different reasons. Flip-flops or shoes are great for the beach, the pool, or relaxing walks. Sneakers or hiking shoes are good for outdoor activities like climbing, biking, or traveling. Dress shoes or flats are nice for eating out, dancing, or visiting events.

Accessories

- Hat and sunglasses are important to protect your eyes and face from the sun's rays. Choose a hat that has a wide top and fits well. Choose sunglasses that have U.V. protection and fit your face shape.

- **Sunscreen:** You'll need sunscreen with a high SPF to avoid sunburns and skin damage. Choose a water-resistant, reef-safe sunscreen, and good for your skin type.

- **Insect repellent:** You'll need insect repellent to ward off mosquitoes and sand fleas, especially if it's been raining recently or if you're coming during the wet season. Choose a bug protection that includes DEET, picaridin, or oil of lemon eucalyptus.

- **Umbrella or rain jacket:** You'll need an umbrella or a rain jacket to keep you dry in a quick shower or storm. Choose an umbrella that is small, lightweight, and strong. Choose a rain jacket that is waterproof, comfortable, and packable.

- **Beach bag:** You'll need a beach bag to take your items to and from the beach. Choose a beach bag that is roomy, sturdy, and easy to clean.

Other Items

- **Passport:** You'll need a legal passport to enter Turks and Caicos. Ensure your passport has at least six months of validity before your trip. You may also need a visa based on your country. Check the visa conditions before your journey.

- **Camera:** You'll want to record the beauty and memories of your trip with a camera. Choose a camera that is high-quality, easy to use, and waterproof. You may also want extra batteries, memory cards, and tools.

- **Snorkeling equipment:** If you love snorkeling, you should bring it instead of buying it on the Island. This way, you can ensure that your equipment fits well, works well, and is clean. Consider bringing an underwater camera or a GoPro to record your underwater experiences.

- **Food items:** If you have any dietary restrictions or preferences, you may want to bring some food items to supplement your meals on the Island. You can bring snacks, bars, nuts, dried fruits, granola, tea bags, coffee packets, spices, sauces, or anything non-perishable and easy to pack.

- **More cash:** While most places on the Island accept credit cards or U.S. dollars, it's always good to have some cash on hand for tips, cabs, small purchases, or emergencies. You can swap your cash at the airport, a bank, or an A.T.M. on the Island.

Now that you know what to pack for your Turks and Caicos trip, here are some tips and tricks to make your packing process easier and more efficient.

- **Make a packing list:** Before you start packing, list everything you need to bring. This will help you avoid losing anything important or packing useless things.

You can use this guide as a reference or make your list based on your wants and tastes.

- **Check the weather:** Before you pack, check the weather report for your trip plans and location. This will help you pack the right clothes and items for the expected weather. You can also check the past weather data for the month to get a general idea of what to expect.

- **Pack in layers:** Packing in layers is a smart way to adapt to changing weather and temperatures. You can layer your clothes to add or remove warmth as needed. For example, you can wear a T-shirt, a sweater, and a jacket and then take off or put on each layer based on how hot or cold you feel.

- **Roll your clothes:** Rolling your clothes is a space-saving method that can help you fit more things in your bag. It can also avoid wrinkles and folds in your clothes. To roll your clothes, fold them in half lengthwise, then roll them tightly from the bottom up. You can then stack them upright or crosswise in your bag.

- **Use packing cubes:** Packing cubes are small bags that help you organize and compress your things. You can use them to sort your clothes by type, color, or outfit. You can also use them to store your belongings, toiletries, electronics, or any other things that need to be grouped. Packing boxes make finding what you need easier and keeping your bag neat and clean.

- **Pack smart:** Pack smart by following some easy rules and tips. For example, pack the biggest items at the bottom of your bag and the lightest items at the top. Pack the things you'll need first or often at the top or in an open bag. Pack drinks, gels, and sprays in a clear plastic bag and place them in an easy-to-reach spot. Pack jewels, papers, medicines, and basics in your carry-on bag. Pack some extra plastic bags for dirty clothes, wet swimsuits, or trash. Pack some extra room for gifts or shopping.

Visa and entry requirements

Turks and Caicos is a British Overseas Territory that accepts tourists from all over the world. However, before you pack your bags and head to this tropical paradise, you'll need to make sure you have the right papers and meet the entry standards.

Passport

You'll need a legal visa to enter Turks and Caicos, regardless of your country or method of transportation. Your passport must be good for at least six months beyond your planned travel date and have at least two blank pages. Children under 16 can travel on their parents' papers unless they are going through the U.S.

Visa

Most tourists do not need a visa to enter Turks and Caicos for vacation if they have a current passport and a return or onward ticket. This applies to people from more than 100 countries and regions, including the US, Canada, the U.K., the E.U., Australia, New Zealand, Japan, China, Brazil and many more. You can check the list of visa-exempt countries on the official government website.

If you are not from a visa-exempt country, you must apply for a visitor's visa before your journey. You can do this online or at the nearest British High Commission, Embassy or Consulate, or the Director of Immigration in Grand Turk. You'll need to provide:

- A filled application form
- Two passport-sized pictures approved by a Justice of the Peace
- A recent police record from your place of birth (translation if not in English)
- A job letter (or proof of business license if self-employed)
- A bank reference letter
- Your passport
- A copy of your surety's identification (signed)
- A closing letter from your surety asking for a visa on your behalf
- A school letter for children
- Evidence of your legal position in your country of residence

- Evidence of your surety's legal standing in Turks and Caicos
- An processing fee of $100 (non-refundable)
- An extra fee of $150 upon approval

The visitor's visa allows you to stay in Turks and Caicos for up to 90 days but does not permit you to work or study.

COVID-19

As of May 1st, 2022, all tourists aged 18 and over must show proof of vaccination against COVID-19 and hold a round-trip ticket. No T.C.I. Assured Portal, insurance or COVID test is needed. However, you should still check the latest health information and flight limits before your journey, as they may change anytime.

Tips and Advice

- Ensure your passport is current and has enough blank pages before leaving.
- Check if you need a visa, and apply well in advance if you do.
- Always carry a copy of your passport, visa and vaccine proof with you.

- Keep your visa and customs papers until you leave the country.
- Follow the rules and laws of Turks and Caicos and accept the local culture and habits.
- Enjoy your stay in Turks and Caicos!

Duration of Stay

Visitors may be allowed entry for up to 90 days, based on their nationality and reason of stay. However, usually, entry is given for 30 days only, even if you have a return ticket for a later date. If you want to continue your stay, you'll need to visit an office of the Immigration Department and pay for an extension. The fee is $50 for the first 90 days and $100 for each subsequent 90 days.

It would help if you did not overstay your visa or entry stamp, as this may result in fines, removal or a ban from re-entering Turks and Caicos. You should also not work or study on a vacation visa or entry stamp, which may lead to legal implications.

Customs and Duty-Free Allowances

When you arrive in Turks and Caicos, you must clear customs and report any goods there. You can bring in $600 worth of things duty-free, including gifts, souvenirs, personal belongings and drinks. Anything over this amount will be subject to duty and taxes.

Some things, such as drugs, plants, animals and protected species, are banned or restricted. You'll need a signed authorization from the officials to bring in these things. You should also avoid bringing in any food items that may pose a health risk or break local laws.

When you leave Turks and Caicos, you'll need to follow the customs laws of your target country.

Summary

Turks and Caicos is a friendly location that gives visa-free entry to most tourists for vacation reasons. You'll need a legal visa, a return or onward ticket, and proof of vaccination against COVID-19. You can stay for up to 90 days, but you may need to ask for an extension if you want to stay longer. You should obey the customs and duty-free limits and avoid bringing in or taking out any banned or limited things.

Currency and Language in Turks and Caicos

Turks and Caicos is a British Overseas Territory that consists of 40 islands and cays in the Caribbean. The islands are popular for tourists who want to enjoy the beautiful beaches, reefs, and wildlife. Before you visit Turks and Caicos, it's important to know some general information about the economy and language of the islands, as well as some tips on how to get around and speak with the people. Here are some things you should know about cash and language in Turks and Caicos.

Currency

The official currency of Turks and Caicos is the U.S. Dollar (USD). This means you don't need to switch your money before or after landing on the islands, as all prices are quoted in USD, and all companies accept USD as payment. You can also use your credit or debit cards at most places, but some may charge a fee or a higher exchange rate. Having some cash on hand for tips, cabs, or small purchases is always a good idea.

There are no foreign exchange or Bureau de Change services at the airport or anywhere else on the islands, except for local banks. However, swapping cash at local banks is not advised, as they offer very poor rates and long waiting times. If you need to swap cash, it's better to do it before you arrive in Turks and Caicos.

There are also no ATMs at the airport, but you can find them at big food shops, motels, and gas stops on the islands. However, A.T.M.s are often out of service or out of cash, so don't depend on them as your only source of money. If you see a working A.T.M., it's wise to use it while you can. Also, check with your bank or card provider about the fees and rates for taking money from ATMs in Turks and Caicos.

Turks and Caicos also mint its coins called Crowns, which show different animals or images of the islands on one side, and the Queen on the other side. These coins are equal to USD (1 Crown = 1 USD), but they are not used as real cash. They are mostly offered as keepsakes or collectibles; you are unlikely to meet them in traffic. If you do receive any Crowns as change, you can exchange them at the Treasury or keep them as a keepsake.

Language

The official language of Turks and Caicos is English, which almost everyone on the islands speaks. This makes it easy for tourists to interact with the people and understand signs, options, and directions. However, you may also hear some forms of English spoken by different groups of people on the islands, such as Turks and Caicos Creole (a dialect influenced by African languages), Jamaican Patois (a dialect influenced by Spanish and French), or Haitian Creole (a language evolved from French).

Most locals are friendly and helpful and will enjoy your efforts to learn some simple words or sentences in their language. Here are some examples of common words or phrases that you may hear or use on the islands:

- Hello: Hello
- Goodbye: Goodbye
- Thank you: Thank you
- Please: Please
- Yes: Yes
- No: No
- How are you?: How are you?

- I'm fine: I'm fine
- What is your name?: What is your name?
- My name is...: My name is...
- Where are you from?: Where are you from?
- I'm from...: I'm from...
- How much is this?: How much is this?
- Do you speak English?: Do you speak English?
- I don't understand: I don't understand
- Excuse me: Excuse me
- Sorry: Sorry
- Cheers: Cheers
- Enjoy your meal: Enjoy your meal
- Have a nice day: Have a nice day

These are some of the things you should know about cash and language in Turks and Caicos. This part will help you with your trip guide project. Have a wonderful day!

Suggested Budget

Turks and Caicos is a dream location for many tourists, with its gorgeous beaches, blue waves, and diverse marine life. However, it is also known as one of the most pricey islands in the Caribbean, with high housing, food, and sports prices. But don't let that stop you from visiting this beautiful place. With some planning and smart tips, you can enjoy Turks and Caicos on a budget and have an amazing holiday.

How to Save on Flights to Turks and Caicos

The trip is one of the biggest costs of going to Turks and Caicos. The Island's largest airport is Providenciales International Airport (P.L.S.), which gets direct flights from several big places in the US, Canada, and Europe. However, these trips can be pricey, especially during the peak season from December to April.

To save money on trips, here are some tips:

- Be open with your times and locations. You can use tools like Skyscanner or Google Flights to check prices across different times and cities. Sometimes, going to a close island like Puerto Rico or Dominican

Republic and then taking a connecting trip to Turks and Caicos can be cheaper than flying straight.

- Sign up for flight updates and deals. You can use sites like FareDrop or Scott's Cheap Trips to get warned of cheap trips to Turks and Caicos. These deals can be gone quickly, so be ready to book when you see them.

- Use points or miles to book your flight. If you have a travel credit card or a frequent flyer program, you can use your points or miles to purchase flights to Turks and Caicos. This can save you a lot of money, especially if you book during off-peak times or use partner flights.

How to Save on Accommodation in Turks and Caicos

Another big cost of going to Turks and Caicos is lodging. The Island is known for its upscale resorts and houses, which can cost hundreds or even thousands of dollars per night. However, budget tourists also have cheaper choices, such as guesthouses, flats, or dorms.

To save money on lodging, here are some tips:

1. Book in advance or last minute. Depending on the season and availability, you can find better deals by booking your hotel in advance or at the last minute. You can use sites like Booking.com or Airbnb to compare costs and reviews across different homes.

2. Stay away from Grace Bay. Grace Bay is the most famous and expensive place in Turks and Caicos, with its beautiful beach and upscale resorts. However, other places are cheaper and still offer beautiful views and access to the beach, such as Long Bay, Turtle Cove, or Leeward.

3. Share your stay with others. If you go with friends or family, you can split the cost of getting a house or an apartment. This can be cheaper than sleeping in different hotel rooms and also give you more space and services. You can also try Couchsurfing or living in a hotel room if you are solo or are okay sharing with strangers.

How to Save on Food and Drinks in Turks and Caicos

Food and drinks in Turks and Caicos can also be quite expensive, especially if you eat at restaurants or bars daily. The Island's food is inspired by its past and culture, having meals like conch cakes, jerk chicken, crab curry, or fish tacos. However, these meals can also be pricey, especially if they include fish or foreign products.

To save money on food and drinks, here are some tips:

1. Cook your meals or buy food. If you stay in a hotel with a kitchen or a fridge, you can cook meals or buy groceries from local stores or markets. This can save you much money compared to going out every day. You can buy food and drinks from grocery shops or gas stations instead of hotel minibars or vending machines.

2. Eat at neighborhood places or food trucks. If you want to try the local cuisine without breaking the bank, you can eat at local eateries or food trucks that

serve real and delicious meals at reasonable prices. You can find these places along the main roads or near famous sites. Some examples are Da Conch Shack, Turks Kebab, Cocovan, and Miss B's Restaurant.

3. Drink local beer or rum punch. To enjoy a drink in Turks and Caicos, you can save money by having local beer or rum punch instead of foreign wine or cocktails. The local beer, Turk's Head, comes in different types like lager, brown ale, or I.P.A. The drink has local rum, fruit juice, grenadine, and spices.

How to Save on Activities in Turks and Caicos

Turks and Caicos offers a range of tourist activities, from relaxing on the beach to exploring the underground world. However, some activities can be expensive, especially if they involve tool rental, tour guides, or entry fees. However, there are also some free or cheap things that you can enjoy in Turks and Caicos, such as:

1. Snorkeling. Turks and Caicos have some of the best diving spots in the Caribbean, with clear water, beautiful coral reefs, and diverse marine life. You can swim for free at some of the public sites, such as Bight Beach, Smith's Reef, or Coral Gardens. You can also rent diving gear from local shops or hotels for a small fee.

2. Hiking. Turks and Caicos has some beautiful hike trails that offer stunning views of the Island and its nature. You can hike for free at some of the national parks or natural areas, such as Chalk Sound National Park, Northwest Point National Park, or Crossing Place Trail. You can also join organized hikes for a small fee from local companies or organizations.

3. Kayaking or paddle boarding. Turks and Caicos have some quiet, flat waters that are great for kayaking or paddle boarding. You can kayak or paddle board for free if you stay at a hotel or lodge with complimentary tools. You can also rent boats or paddle boards from local shops or companies for a small fee.

Suggested Budget for Turks and Caicos

Based on the tips above, here is a possible price for a 7-day trip to Turks and Caicos for two people in 2023-2024:

- Flights: $830 ($415 per person)
- Accommodation: $700 ($100 per night)
- Food and drinks: $490 ($35 per person per day)
- Activities: $280 ($20 per person per day)
- Total: $2300 ($1150 per person)

This budget is based on an average or reasonable spending, but you can change it according to your tastes and needs. You can also use tools like Where And When to determine your trip spending and cost of living in Turks and Caicos.

Turks and Caicos is a beautiful and expensive island spot, but it doesn't have to be out of reach for budget tourists. With some planning and smart tips, you can enjoy Turks and Caicos on a budget and have an amazing holiday.

To conclude, Turks and Caicos is a paradise for tourists who love beaches, nature, and culture. However, it can also be an expensive location, especially during the peak season. But with some planning and smart tips, you can visit Turks and Caicos on a budget and have a great holiday. You can save money on flights, lodgings, food and drinks, and events without losing on quality or fun. Turks and Caicos is a place worth saving for and going at least once in your lifetime.

Money saving tips

Turks and Caicos is a dream location for many tourists who want to experience the Caribbean's beauty, culture and excitement. However, it is also known as one of the most pricey places in the area, with high costs for flights, lodging, food, sports and transportation. But don't let that stop you from visiting this paradise. There are many ways to save money and enjoy Turks and Caicos on a budget. Here are some tips and tricks to help you plan your trip without breaking the bank.

Book cheap flights

The first step to saving money on your Turks and Caicos trip is to find cheap tickets. The main airport in Turks and Caicos is the Providenciales International Airport (P.L.S.), which gets flights from different places in the United States, Canada, the United Kingdom, the Caribbean and other countries. You can also find holidays or special trips from other locations.

You need to be open with your times, locations and carriers to find cheap trips. You can use internet tools such as Skyscanner, Kayak or Google Flights to compare costs and choices. You can also sign up for email alerts or newsletters from different flights or travel websites to get informed of deals and savings. You can also use credit card points or miles to buy flights or get cash back.

Some of the carriers that fly to Turks and Caicos are:

- **American Airlines:** from Miami, Charlotte, Philadelphia, New York (J.F.K.), Boston, Chicago (O'Hare) and Dallas (Fort Worth).
- **Delta Air Lines:** from Atlanta, New York (J.F.K.) and Boston.
- **JetBlue Airways:** from New York (J.F.K.), Boston, Fort Lauderdale and Newark.
- **United Airlines:** from Newark, Houston (Intercontinental) and Chicago (O'Hare).

- **Southwest Airlines:** from Baltimore, Fort Lauderdale and Houston (Hobby).
- **Air Canada:** from Toronto, Montreal and Ottawa.
- **WestJet:** from Toronto.
- **British Airways:** from London (Gatwick) via Antigua.
- **InterCaribbean Airways:** from Antigua, Bahamas (Nassau), Cuba (Havana), Dominican Republic (Santo Domingo), Haiti (Port-au-Prince), Jamaica (Kingston) and Puerto Rico (San Juan).
- **Caicos Express Airways:** from Bahamas (Nassau) and Dominican Republic (Santiago).
- **Bahamasair:** from Bahamas (Nassau).

Choose affordable housing

The second step to saving money on your Turks and Caicos trip is to choose cheap lodging. The most famous and expensive place to stay in Turks and Caicos is Grace Bay Beach on Providenciales, where you can find luxury resorts, houses and condos with beautiful ocean views. However, other choices are more budget-friendly and offer warmth, ease and charm.

You can stay outside of Grace Bay Beach in other places of Providenciales, such as Turtle Cove, Leeward, Long Bay or Chalk Sound. You can also stay on other islands of Turks and Caicos, such as Grand Turk, Salt Cay, South Caicos or North Caicos. You can find smaller hotels, guesthouses, cottages or flats that offer basic services, local culture and access to beaches and sites.

You can also use online platforms such as Airbnb, VRBO or Booking.com to find private homes that fit your wants and tastes. You can also use credit card points or miles to claim lodging or get cash back.

Some of the cheap lodging choices in Turks and Caicos are:

- **La Vista Azul Resort:** a 3-star hotel in Turtle Cove with a pool, a restaurant and a spa.
- **Ports of Call Resort:** a 3-star hotel in Grace Bay with a pool, a restaurant and a bus service.
- **Osprey Beach Hotel:** a 3-star hotel in Grand Turk with a pool, a restaurant and a dive shop.
- **Sailrock Resort:** a 4-star resort in South Caicos with a pool, a restaurant and a spa.

- **Pelican Beach Hotel:** a 2-star hotel in North Caicos with a kitchen and a beach entrance.

Cook your meals.

The third step to saving money on your Turks and Caicos trip is to cook your food. Eating out in Turks and Caicos can be very expensive, especially if you eat at places with ocean views or tourist meals. However, there are also ways to save money on food while maintaining quality and taste.

You can cook your own food at your hotel if you have access to a kitchen or kitchenette. You can buy food at area stores, such as Graceway I.G.A., Quality Supermarket or Smart Grocery. You can also buy fresh vegetables, meat, fish and made goods at local markets, such as the Island Fish Fry, the Farmers Market or the Bakery. You can also buy snacks, drinks and groceries at convenience shops like Caicos Express or Rubis.

You can also eat out at cheaper places like food trucks, shops, pubs or bars. You can find local favorites, such as conch cakes, jerk chicken, peas and rice or rum cake. You can also find foreign foods, such as pizza, burgers, sushi or tacos. You can also take advantage of happy hours, deals or savings at some places and bars.

Some of the cheap places to eat in Turks and Caicos are:

- **Turks Kebab:** a Grace Bay food truck serving Turkish and Mediterranean meals.
- Da Conch Shack is a seaside restaurant in Blue Hills serving conch and fish meals.
- **Chinson's Grill Shack:** a roadside restaurant on Leeward Highway that serves Chinese and Caribbean foods.
- **Jack's Shack:** a seaside bar in Grand Turk that serves burgers, snacks and drinks.
- **Last Chance Bar and Grill:** a South Caicos seaside diner serving local and foreign foods.

Rent a car or bike.

The fourth step to saving money on your Turks and Caicos trip is to rent a car or bike. Transportation in Turks and Caicos can be expensive, especially if you rely on cabs or groups. However, there are also ways to save money on transportation without missing out on the sights and activities.

You can take a car or bike to explore the islands at your own pace and ease. You can find hire companies at the airport or in town that offer different types of vehicles, such as cars, jeeps, bikes or bicycles. You can also use credit card points or miles to claim rentals or get cash back.

You can also use public transportation or hitching to get around the islands. Some cars or jitneys run along the main roads of Providenciales and Grand Turk. Some boats join some islands, such as Providenciales and North Caicos. You can also hitchhike with locals or tourists ready to give you a ride.

Some of the hiring companies in Turks and Caicos are:

- Grace Bay Car Rentals: a car hire service in Providenciales that offers free airport pickup and drop-off.
- Tony's Car Rental: a car rental service in Grand Turk that offers free delivery and return.

- Scooter Bob's: a car and bike rental business in Turtle Cove that offers free maps and help.
- Big Blue Collective: a bike hire service in Leeward that offers guided trips and tracks.
- Caribbean Cruisin': a boat service between Providenciales and North Caicos.

Pack smart

Packaging smart is the fifth step to saving money on your Turks and Caicos trip. Packing smart means taking only what you need and avoiding needless fees or costs. However, it also means being prepared for any situation or disaster that may happen.

You can pack smart by following these tips:

- Check the weather prediction and pack accordingly. Turks and Caicos has a tropical climate with warm and sunny days year-round. However, it can also experience rain showers, storms or cold fronts. Pack light clothes, swimming, sunglasses, sunscreen, hat, umbrella and jacket.

- Check the baggage limit and fees of your flight and pack accordingly. Turks and Caicos has strict customs rules on what you can bring into the country. Pack only necessary things, such as toiletries, medicines, papers, gadgets and jewels. Avoid taking forbidden things like guns, drugs, plants or animals.

- Check the services and features of your lodgings and pack accordingly. Turks and Caicos have different levels of ease and convenience based on where you stay. Pack things that may not be given or expensive, such as towels, sheets, blankets, soap, shampoo, water bottles, snacks and drinks.

- Check the events and sites of your schedule and pack accordingly. Turks and Caicos have various things to do and see based on your hobbies and tastes. Pack things that may improve your experience or may be needed for safety or security reasons, such as camera, binoculars, such as cameras, binoculars, diving gear, reef-safe sunscreen, insect protection, first aid kit and flashlight.

By packing smart, you can save on travel fees, customs taxes, shopping expenses and emergency costs. You can also enjoy your trip more easily and boldly.

Turks and Caicos is a location that can be enjoyed by any means. Following these tips and tricks can save money and still have a unique and amazing trip. You can enjoy the best of Turks and Caicos without spending a lot.

Best places to book your trip

Turks and Caicos is a popular location for tourists who want to enjoy the beauty and peace of the Caribbean. Whether you're looking for a romantic break, a family vacation, or an adventure-filled escape, you must book your trip in advance to secure the best deals and access. Here are some of the best places to book your trip to Turks and Caicos.

Booking.com

Booking.com is one of the main online travel sites that offer a wide range of lodging choices, from hotels and cabins to flats and houses. You can compare costs, read reviews, see pictures, and check availability for over 150 homes in Turks and Caicos. You can filter your search by area, star grade, price, amenities, etc. Booking.com offers free refunds on most plans, 24/7 customer service, and safe payment methods. You can book your trip on Booking.com's website or app.

Expedia

Expedia is another online travel site that provides lodging, flights, car rentals, sports, and holiday packages. You can book everything you need for your trip in one place and save money and time. Expedia also offers rewards points, exclusive deals, and flexible payment choices. You can book your trip on Expedia's website or app.

Beaches Turks & Caicos

Beaches Turks & Caicos is an all-inclusive resort with a luxury and family-friendly experience on Grace Bay Beach. The resort features roomy rooms and suites, a gym, a water park, a golf course, a kids' club, and several eating choices. The resort also includes endless water sports, land sports, entertainment, and airport transfers. You can book your trip on Beaches Turks & Caicos' website or by phone.

Turks & Caicos Reservations

Turks & Caicos Reservations is a local travel service specializing in creating trips to Turks and Caicos. The agency has a team of experts who can help you find the best housing, flights, activities, and deals for your wants and interests. The service also offers secret tips, local information, and exclusive deals. You can book your trip on the Turks & Caicos Reservations' website or by phone.

Booking your trip to Turks and Caicos can be easy and convenient if you use one of the best places to book your trip. Whether you prefer an online travel site, an all-inclusive vacation, or a local travel service, you can find the best deals and access for your trip. You can also enjoy the perks of customer service, awards, and freedom. No matter how you book your trip, you'll surely have an amazing time in Turks and Caicos.

CHAPTER 2

TURKS AND CAICOS TOP ATTRACTIONS

Turks and Caicos is a stunning archipelago of 40 islands and cays in the Caribbean, known for its clean beaches, blue waters, and rich marine life. Whether looking for relaxation, excitement, culture, or history, you'll find plenty of sites to fit your tastes and price. Here are some top sites in Turks and Caicos that you should take advantage of on your trip.

Grace Bay Beach

Grace Bay Beach is the crown jewel of Turks and Caicos and one of the most beautiful beaches in the world. This 12-mile (19-km) stretch of soft white sand and clear blue water is great for swimming, relaxing, fishing, kayaking, or enjoying the scenery. Grace Bay Beach is also home to many resorts, restaurants, shops, and activities, making it a handy and exciting base for your holiday. You can also explore the nearby Bight Reef, a coral garden that hosts a variety of bright fish and sea turtles.

Chalk Sound National Park

Chalk Sound National Park is a natural beauty that will take your breath away. This protected area covers thousands of acres of water with over 350 small islands, surrounded by water that is so clear and bright that it looks like liquid chalk. You can rent a kayak or paddleboard to explore the islands or take a boat tour to see the wildlife, such as iguanas, flamingos, pelicans, and stingrays. Chalk Sound National Park is also close to two other amazing beaches: Taylor Bay Beach and Sapodilla Bay Beach, which have quiet and small waves ideal for families with children.

Cockburn Town

Cockburn Town is the capital of Turks and Caicos and is located on Grand Turk, the largest Island in the group. This beautiful town has a rich history and culture that goes back to the 17th century when it was a major salt-producing center and a stopover for travelers and pirates. You can stroll along the narrow streets lined with colonial buildings, visit the Turks and Caicos National Museum to learn about the Island's history and shipwrecks or enjoy the local food at one of the many bars and restaurants. Cockburn Town is also a great place to experience the Island's nightlife, with live music and dancing at different spots.

Humpback Whales

One of the most exciting sights in Turks and Caicos is the chance to see humpback whales in their native environment. Every year, from January to April, thousands of these beautiful creatures pass through the seas of Turks and Caicos on their way to their breeding grounds in the Dominican Republic. You can take a whale-watching tour to get close to these gentle giants or even swim or dive with them if you're lucky. You'll be amazed by their size, ease, and songs as they interact with each other.

Grand Turk Lighthouse

Grand Turk Lighthouse is a historic icon that offers amazing views of the Island and the water. Built-in 1852 by British builders, this 60-foot (18-m) tall building was intended to prevent accidents on the dangerous rocks around Grand Turk. Today, you can climb up the spiral stairs to the top of the tower and enjoy the sweeping view or visit the nearby museum that shows items and photos from the Island's past. You can also explore the nearby areas, where you'll find donkeys, horses, cows, and birds.

The Hole

The Hole is a mystery draw that will interest daring visitors. Located on Providenciales, this natural feature is a big sinkhole that drops about 50 feet (15 m) into the ground. You can reach The Hole by walking along a dirt road off Leeward Highway or by taking an organized tour that will provide safety tools and nets. Once you reach The Hole, you can look into its depths or even fall into it if you're brave enough. You'll find a secret cave with stalactites and stalagmites and an underground lake.

Snorkeling and Diving

Turks and Caicos is a paradise for snorkeling and diving lovers, as it boasts one of the longest coral reefs in the world and a wealth of marine life. You can snorkel or dive at many sites around the islands, such as Smith's Reef, Coral Gardens, Malcolm's Road Beach, Northwest Point Marine National Park, Salt Cay Divers, and West Caicos Wall. You'll be amazed by the variety and beauty of the coral formations, sponges, sea fans, and marine animals, such as sharks, rays, turtles, dolphins, and crabs. You can also visit some ships on the ocean floor, such as the Endymion and the H.M.S. Trouvadore.

Caicos Conch Farm

Caicos Conch Farm is a unique site that displays the national sign and threat of Turks and Caicos: the conch. This farm is the only one of its kind in the world, and it grows and raises Caribbean queen conchs for food and protection. You can take a guided walk of the facility and learn about the life cycle and biology of these interesting mollusks and see them in different stages of growth. You can also meet the two resident conchs, Sally and Jerry, who will show their skills and traits.

Cheshire Hall Plantation

Cheshire Hall Plantation is a historical place that offers a glimpse into the Island's colonial past. This farm was built in the late 18th century by a conservative family from South Carolina who fled to Turks and Caicos after the American Revolution. The farm grew cotton, sisal, and animals and worked hundreds of enslaved Africans. Today, you can explore the remains of the estate house, kitchen, cisterns, walls, and slave cells and take in the scenery of the surrounding area. You can also visit the nearby Wade's Green Plantation, another Republican house that has been protected as a national park.

Gibbs Cay

Gibbs Cay is a small empty island famous for its friendly stingrays. You can take a boat trip to this Island from Grand Turk or Salt Cay and swim with these gentle creatures in the shallow water. The stingrays are used for human contact and will swim up to you for food and petting. You can also relax on the white sand beach, eat under the palm trees, or hike to the top of the Island for sweeping views.

Mangrove Cay

Mangrove Cay is a big island that is part of the Princess Alexandra National Park on Providenciales. This Island is covered with green mangrove woods that provide a vital home for many birds, fish, crabs, and snakes. You can explore Mangrove Cay by kayak or paddle board and find the secret waterways and ponds that teem with life. You'll see pelicans, herons, egrets, ospreys, lemon sharks, barracudas, snappers, crabs, conchs, and more. Mangrove Cay is also a great place to watch the sunset over the water.

Turks and Caicos is a location that offers something for everyone, from beautiful beaches and reefs to historical and cultural sites. Whether you want to relax, explore, or learn, you'll find plenty of sites to fill your schedule and make your trip unique. Take the chance to experience the beauty and variety of this Caribbean paradise. Book your trip to Turks and Caicos today and find out why it's one of the best places to visit in the world.

CHAPTER 3

TURKS AND CAICOS'S BEST RESTAURANTS AND CAFES

Turks and Caicos is a paradise for food lovers, with various foods and tastes to fit every palate. Whether you're looking for a romantic dinner, a casual lunch, or a quick bite, you'll find plenty of choices to fill your needs. Based on scores, reviews, and popularity, here are some of the best restaurants and bars in Turks and Caicos for 2023-2024.

Turks and Caicos offers various eating choices, from traditional cuisine to foreign meals inspired by tastes worldwide.

In this chapter, we will explore some of the best restaurants and bars in Turks and Caicos, including famous places which are known for their original meals, excellent service, and unique ambiance.

So, join us as we start a culinary trip through the lively and delicious Island of Turks and Caicos.

Traditional Turks and Caicos Restaurants

Turks and Caicos is not only a paradise for beach lovers but also for foodies who want to taste the flavors of the Caribbean. The islands offer various eating choices, from casual crab shacks to elegant restaurants, where you can enjoy fresh fish, local favorites, and foreign cuisine. Whether you're looking for a romantic dinner under the stars, a family-friendly spot with a view, or a secret gem off the beaten path, you'll find it in Turks and Caicos. Here are some of the best traditional places in the archipelago where you can savor this tropical location's original foods and atmosphere.

Da Conch Shack

Da Conch Shack is one of the most famous places in Turks and Caicos and, possibly, the entire West Indies. Located on the beach in Blue Hills, this relaxed eatery serves conch in all its forms: split, frittered, boiled, roasted, and more. You can also try other seafood treats, such as lobster, jerk ribs, and fish tacos, or opt for veggie choices like curry or salad. The diner has a laid-back vibe, with live music, colorful art, and friendly staff. You can eat under the palm trees, watch the waves roll in, and even pick your conch from the water.

Da Conch Shack is a must-visit for anyone who wants to experience the true spirit of Turks and Caicos food.

Coco Bistro

Coco Bistro is the right setting for a chic, sophisticated evening out on the island of Providenciales. Located in the biggest palm tree on the island, the restaurant offers a beautiful environment with sparkling lights, soft music, and a gentle breeze. The menu features unique recipes with the best local and foreign ingredients, such as mahi-mahi with mango salsa, West Indian-style shrimp curry, pepper-crusted tuna with melon salsa, and a rack of lamb with mint sauce. You can also enjoy a range of good wines and drinks to complement your food. Coco Bistro is one of the most popular places in Turks and Caicos, so book your table in advance.

Coco Bistro

Bay Bistro

Bay Bistro is another elegant (and romantic) choice for eating beneath the trees of Providenciales—although this time, your meal will also view the Caribbean Sea. The restaurant is situated on Grace Bay Beach, at the Sibonné Beach Hotel, and offers a beautiful view of the blue water and white sand. The menu offers fresh seafood and meat meals with a Caribbean flair, such as conch soup, lobster thermidor, coconut curry chicken, and filet mignon with blue cheese sauce. You can also partake in rich treats like chocolate cake, key lime pie, or coconut cream brulee. Bay Bistro is especially famous for its seaside barbecue nights on Wednesdays and Sundays, where you can enjoy live music and entertainment while dining on grilled favourites.

Bay Bistro

Hemingway's Restaurant

Hemingway's restaurant is named after the famous writer who visited Turks and Caicos in the 1930s. The eatery respects his memory with a friendly setting, old photos, and quotes on the walls. The menu offers a range of meals inspired by Hemingway's trips worldwide, such as Cuban sandwiches, Spanish paella, Moroccan lamb tagine, and French onion soup. You can also find neighbourhood favourites like crab cakes, cracked lobster tail, spicy chicken pasta, and grouper almondine. Hemingway's restaurant is at The Sands at Grace Bay Resort, facing the beach and pool. It's open for breakfast, lunch, and dinner daily.

Sj's Curry Club

Sj's Curry Club is the place to go if you want some spice. This secret gem in Providenciales serves real Indian food with a Caribbean twist. There are several soups to select from, tandoori meals, biryanis, and naan bread, all made with fresh vegetables and aromatic spices. You can also adjust your amount of heat from mild to extra hot. Sj's Curry Club is situated in a small area near Grace Bay Road and has a simple but cosy interior. Starting on Tuesday, the restaurant is open for lunch and supper to Saturday and also gives takeout and delivery choices.

Sj's Curry Club

Turks Kebab

Turks Kebab is another great choice for filling your hunger with delicious and cheap food. This family-owned restaurant in Providenciales serves Mediterranean and Turkish foods, such as kebabs, gyros, falafel, hummus, soups, and pies. You can order your food as a wrap, a plate, or a salad and enjoy it with handmade sauces and bread. Turks Kebab also has a range of desserts, drinks, and shakes to finish your meal. The diner has a relaxed and friendly setting, with indoor and outdoor seats. It's open for lunch and dinner every day except Sundays.

Turks Kebab

Caribbean Element

Caribbean Element is a modern and stylish restaurant that celebrates the variety and blend of Caribbean food. The restaurant in Grace Bay Plaza has a sleek and roomy interior with bright highlights. The menu features meals that blend traditional and modern tastes, such as jerk pork belly with pineapple salsa, coconut curry fish with plantain mash, lobster mac and cheese with truffle oil, and roasted oxtail with rice and peas. You can also enjoy drinks, wines, beers, and mocktails to pair with your food. Caribbean Element is open for dinner from Tuesday to Saturday.

Caribbean Element

Cocovan

Cocovan is a fun and quirky idea that offers delicious street food from an old airstream trailer. The trailer is parked next to Coco Bistro in Providenciales and serves a range of great meals for sharing or eating. You can find tacos, burgers, sliders, soups, fries, wings, and more made with fresh and local products. You can also treat yourself to some ice cream or cookies for dinner. Cocovan has a lively vibe, with music, lights, and outdoor seats. It's open for dinner from Tuesday to Saturday.

Miss B's Restaurant

Miss B's Restaurant is a family-run business that serves traditional Turks and Caicos food on the island of North Caicos. The restaurant is situated in Kew and has a rustic and cosy charm. The menu offers meals made with fresh fish, meat, and food from the island, such as conch cakes, lobster curry, cracked conch, fried chicken, and cooked fish. You can also enjoy fresh treats like chocolate cake, key lime pie, and coconut tart. Miss B's Restaurant is open for lunch and dinner from Monday to Saturday.

Miss B's Restaurant

Arches on the Ridge

Arches on the Ridge is a small cafe offering amazing ocean views and the historic Grand Turk Lighthouse. The cafe is situated on the hill of Grand Turk Island and has lovely decor with arches, wooden furniture, and local artwork. The menu offers choices for breakfast, lunch, and dinner, such as waffles, omelettes, sandwiches, soups, burgers, pasta, and fish. You can also enjoy coffee, tea, shakes, and drinks while enjoying the scenery. Arches on the Ridge is open from Wednesday to Sunday.

<u>Arches on the Ridge</u>

Sea View Cafe

Sea View Cafe is a relaxed and friendly spot that serves wonderful food on the island of Middle Caicos. The bar is at the Blue Horizon Resort, facing Mudjin Harbour Beach. The menu offers local foods such as conch salad, cracked lobster, grilled fish, and jerk chicken. For lighter food, you can also find burgers, pizzas, wraps, and salads. Sea View Cafe has a relaxed setting, with indoor and outdoor seats. It's open for breakfast, lunch, and dinner every day.

These are some of the best classic places in Turks and Caicos, where you can enjoy the tastes and culture of this beautiful location. Whether you're looking for a simple bite, a fancy eating experience, or something in between, you'll find it in Turks and Caicos. Bon appetit!

International Turks and Caicos Restaurants

Turks and Caicos is not only a paradise for beach lovers but also for eaters. The islands offer a wide range of places that serve foreign foods, from Asian and Mediterranean to French and Caribbean. Whether looking for a casual bite or a fancy eating experience, you'll find something to please your taste and cash. Here are some of the best foreign places in Turks and Caicos to try on your trip.

The Grill at Grace Bay Club

The Grill at Grace Bay Club is a chic and classy restaurant that views the beautiful Grace Bay Beach. The menu features modern meals that mix local products with global tastes, such as conch ceviche, lobster risotto, jerk chicken, and grilled mahi-mahi. You can also enjoy various drinks, wines, and beers at the bar or indulge in a treat such as chocolate cake or key lime pie. The Grill is open for breakfast, lunch, and dinner and offers live music on some nights.

Coralli

Coralli is a small private restaurant housed at the Wymara Resort on Grace Bay Beach. The diner specializes in

Mediterranean food, including hummus, falafel, lamb chops, paella, and baklava. You can also enjoy fresh fish, soups, burgers, pies, veggies, and vegan choices. Coralli has a relaxed and beautiful setting, with indoor and outdoor seats, lighting, and ocean views. The restaurant is open for breakfast, lunch, and dinner.

Opus Wine Bar and Grill

Opus Wine Bar and Grill is a classy and stylish restaurant at the Ocean Club Resort on Grace Bay Beach. The restaurant boasts an amazing wine room with over 600 bottles worldwide. The menu features traditional meals with a Caribbean twist, such as conch soup, lobster thermidor, beef tenderloin, and coconut curry shrimp. You can also taste the chef's tasting plate or the daily deals. Opus is open for dinner only, and bookings are suggested.

Sj's Curry Club

Sj's Curry Club is a secret gem that serves traditional Indian food in a relaxed and friendly setting. The restaurant is in a small centre off Leeward Highway and offers take-out and delivery services. The menu includes a range of stews, tandoori meals, biryanis, naan bread, and veggie choices, all made with fresh spices and herbs. Try the chef's specials or the mix plates to taste everything. Sj's Curry Club is open for lunch and dinner.

Caribbean Element

Caribbean Element is a modern and simple restaurant that blends Caribbean tastes with foreign influences. The restaurant at Ports of Call Plaza on Grace Bay Road has indoor and outdoor dining choices. The menu includes:

- Spicy chicken spring rolls
- Coconut curry mussels
- Grilled wahoo steak
- Lamb shank tagine
- Chocolate lava cake

Your meal may be paired with a beverage from the comprehensive wine list or the bar menu. Caribbean Element is open for dinner only.

These are some of the foreign places in Turks and Caicos that you can include in your travel guide part. This draft will help you with your writing job. Have a wonderful day!

Cafes and bakeries

Turks and Caicos is not only heaven for beach lovers but also for coffee and pastry fans. The island has a variety of shops and bakeries that offer wonderful and fresh treats, from espresso and drinks to croissants and cakes. Whether you need a morning boost, a noon snack, or a sweet treat, you'll find plenty of choices to meet your tastes. Based on scores, reviews, and fame, here are some of the best shops and bakeries in Turks and Caicos for 2023-2024.

Shay Cafe & Lounge

Shay Cafe & Lounge is a small, friendly cafe serving breakfast and lunch in Providenciales. The cafe offers a range of meals, such as eggs benedict, banana pancakes, crepes, sandwiches, soups, and burgers. You can also enjoy coffee, tea, shakes, or drinks. The cafe has modern and stylish decor, free Wi-Fi and outdoor seats.

Location: Grace Bay Rd

Lemon2Go Coffee

Lemon2Go Coffee is a lovely shop that serves coffee, tea, drinks, and sweets in Providenciales. The cafe is housed inside a gift shop and a flower shop, providing a cosy and welcoming atmosphere. You may savour your meal and beverage while browsing the selection of gifts, books, candles, and more. The cafe also has free Wi-Fi and outdoor seats.

Location: Grace Bay Rd

Arches on the Ridge

Arches on the Ridge is a small, friendly cafe serving breakfast and lunch in Grand Turk. The cafe is run by Jack and Janet, who make everything from scratch using local foods. You can enjoy meals like wahoo burgers, steak fajita bowls, shrimp tacos, and handmade sweets like key lime pie or chocolate cake. The cafe also has a gift shop to buy items and local crafts.

Location: Cockburn Town

Tribe

The Tribe is a hip and healthy cafe that serves breakfast and lunch in Providenciales. The cafe offers a range of meals, such as granola bowls, avocado toast, wraps, soups, and burgers. You can also enjoy coffee, tea, juice, or kombucha. The cafe has a lively and chic decor, free Wi-Fi and outdoor seats.

Location: Grace Bay Rd

Sea View Cafe

Sea View Cafe is a seaside cafe that serves breakfast and lunch in Middle Caicos. The cafe offers a range of meals, such as omelettes, pancakes, burgers, soups, and fish. You can also enjoy coffee, tea, juice, or beer. The cafe has a rustic and relaxed decor, as well as beautiful views of the ocean.

Location: Bambarra Beach

Turks Wave Cafe

Turks Wave Cafe is a relaxed and fun cafe that serves breakfast and lunch in Providenciales. The cafe offers a range of meals, such as bagels, muffins, burritos, tacos, pies, and soups. You can also enjoy coffee, tea, shakes, or drinks. The cafe has lively, beachy decor, live music, and entertainment.

Location: Grace Bay Rd

Top O' The Cove Deli

Top O', The Cove Deli, is a small and lovely cafe that serves breakfast and lunch in Providenciales. The cafe offers a range of meals, such as French toast, breakfast sandwiches, deli sandwiches, eggs with bacon, and pasta. You can also enjoy coffee, tea, juice, or pop. The cafe has a simple and cosy design and helpful service.

Location: Leeward Highway

Karibae Cafe

Karibae Cafe is a cosy and traditional cafe that serves breakfast and lunch in Providenciales. The cafe offers a range of meals, such as ackee and saltfish, johnny cake, curry goat, jerk chicken, and stew fish. You can also enjoy coffee, tea, juice, or rum punch. The cafe has lively and rustic decor, local artwork and music.

Location: Grace Bay Rd

Cool Beans Cafe

Cool Beans Cafe is a cool and funky cafe that serves breakfast and lunch in Grand Turk. The cafe offers a range of meals, such as waffles, sandwiches, wraps, soups, and burgers. You can also enjoy coffee, tea, smoothies, or drinks. The cafe has quirky and diverse decor, free Wi-Fi and board games.

Location: Duke Street

Moore Fries

Moore Fries is a relaxed and tasty cafe that serves breakfast and lunch in Providenciales. The cafe offers a range of meals, such as fries, hot dogs, burgers, chicken nuggets, and fish fingers. You can also enjoy coffee, tea, juice, or pop. The cafe has simple and clean decor and fast service.

Location: Grace Bay Rd

These are just some of the best shops and bakeries in Turks and Caicos for 2023-2024, but there are many more to find and enjoy. Whether you need a coffee fix, a sugar rush, or a filling meal, you'll find something to fit your taste and price in this island spot.

CHAPTER 4

Turks and Caicos Nightlife and Entertainment

Turks and Caicos may be a paradise for beach lovers, but it also offers plenty for those who want to enjoy fun and excitement after the sun sets. The islands have various nighttime and entertainment choices, from casual bars and pubs to fine restaurants and casinos. Whether you're looking for a lively party, a sweet date, or a cultural event, you'll find it in Turks and Caicos. Here are some of the best bars and entertainment places in the archipelago, where you can experience this tropical location's lively and diverse scene.

Bars and Pubs

Bars and bars are the most popular local way to have a night out in Turks and Caicos. You can find many establishments that serve drinks, food, and music with different atmospheres and themes. Some of the most active nighttime spots are in the Grace Bay area of Providenciales, such as Danny Buoy's Pub and Restaurant, Ricky's on the Beach, Sandbar Restaurant, Somewhere Cafe & Lounge, and The Deck at Seven Stars Resort. These places often have special events like game nights, singing nights, dance nights, and live bands. You can also find some great oceanfront and waterfront bars on other islands, such as Da Conch Shack, Bugaloo's Restaurant, Bob's Bar, and Sharkbite on Providenciales; Arches on the Ridge on Grand Turk; Miss B's Restaurant on North Caicos; Sea View Cafe on Middle Caicos; and The Beached Whale Bar & Grill on Grand Turk.

Beach BBQs and Bonfires

One of the most unique and memorable ways to enjoy the evening in Turks and Caicos is to attend a beach BBQ or bonfire. Motels or restaurants often plan these events and feature delicious food, drinks, music, dancing, fire shows, and fireworks. You can mix with locals and tourists while enjoying the stunning ocean and star views.

Some of the best places to experience a beach BBQ or bonfire are Bay Bistro at Sibonné Beach Hotel on Providenciales; Bohio Dive Resort on Grand Turk; Sailrock Resort on South Caicos; Blue Horizon Resort on Middle Caicos; Parrot Cay Resort on Parrot Cay; The Meridian Club on Pine Cay; The Palms Turks & Caicos on Providenciales; The Sands at Grace Bay on Providenciales; The Shore Club Turks & Caicos on Providenciales; The Somerset on Grace

Bay on Providenciales; West Bay Club on Providenciales; Wymara Resort & Villas on Providenciales.

Live Music

If you love live music, you'll find plenty of places that feature local and foreign talent in Turks and Caicos. You can listen to different types of music, such as reggae, soca, calypso, jazz, blues, rock, and pop. Some of the best places to enjoy live music are Hemingway's Restaurant at The Sands at Grace Bay on Providenciales; Coco Bistro on Providenciales; Cocovan on Providenciales; Danny Buoy's Pub & Restaurant on Providenciales; Grace's Cottage at Point Grace Resort & Spa on Providenciales; Infiniti Restaurant & Raw Bar at Grace Bay Club on Providenciales; Magnolia Wine Bar & Restaurant on Providenciales; Osprey Beach Hotel on Grand Turk; Salt Raker Inn on Grand Turk; The Landing Bar & Kitchen at Blue Haven Resort & Marina on Providenciales; The Regent Village Shopping Center on Providenciales.

Sunset Cruises and Charters

Sunset trips and charters are one of the must-do things in Turks and Caicos. They offer a lovely and relaxed way to enjoy the island's beauty from the water. You can choose from different types of vessels, such as sailboats, catamarans, ships, or party boats. You can also enjoy drinks, snacks, dinner, or entertainment aboard. Some of the best sunset cruises and charters are Atabeyra Sunset Sail on Providenciales; Beluga Sunset Cruise on Providenciales; Big Blue Collective Sunset Cruise on Providenciales; Caicos Dream Tours Sunset Cruise on Providenciales; Island Vibes Tours Sunset Cruise on Providenciales; Kenard Cruises Sunset Cruise on Providenciales; Ocean Vibes Scuba & Watersports Sunset Cruise on Grand Turk; Sail Provo Sunset Sail on Providenciales; Silver Deep Sunset Cruise on Providenciales; Sun Charters Sunset Sail on Providenciales.

Glowworm Cruises

Glowworm tours are another unique and wonderful way to experience the evening in Turks and Caicos. These trips occur around the full moon when the bioluminescent sea worms (Odontosyllis people) perform their breeding routine. The worms emit a green glow that lights the water, creating a beautiful natural event. You can watch this amazing sight from a boat, dive, or swim in the glowing water. Some of the best glowworm cruises are

- Atabeyra Glow Worm Cruise on Providenciales;

- Big Blue Collective Glow Worm Cruise
- Caicos Dream Tours Glow Worm Cruise
- Island Vibes Tours Glow Worm Cruise
- Sail Provo Glow Worm Sail on Providenciales;
- Sun Charters Glow Worm Sail on Providenciales.

Events and Holidays

Turks and Caicos also host yearly events and holidays that offer an amazing and unique experience. The most amazing one is the New Year's Eve fireworks show, one of the biggest in the Caribbean. You can watch the amazing performance from the beach and enjoy live music, dancing, food, and drinks.

Other events and holidays that are worth checking out are the Turks & Caicos Music and Cultural Festival in July, which features local and international artists; the Turks & Caicos Conch Festival in November, which celebrates the national dish of conch; the Turks & Caicos Kite Flying Competition in April, which showcases colourful and creative kites; the Turks & Caicos Carnival in August, which features parades, costumes, music, and dancing; and the

Turks & Caicos International Film Festival in November, which showcases films that promote ocean conservation.

Night Kayaking

If you're feeling brave, you can explore the islands at night on a boat. You can paddle through the calm and clear waters of Chalk Sound National Park or Leeward Channel, where you'll see fish, turtles, stingrays, and other marine life lit by LED lights connected to your kayak. You'll also learn about the history and environment of Turks and Caicos from your guide. This is a fun and eco-friendly way to enjoy the night beauty and wildlife of the islands. Some of the best night kayaking companies are SUP Provo, Silver Deep, and Turks & Caicos Kayaking.

These are some of the best nightlife and entertainment places in Turks and Caicos, where you can have fun and excitement after a day of rest. Whether you're looking for a party, a date, or a cultural event, you'll find it in Turks and Caicos. Enjoy!

CHAPTER 5

SHOPPING IN TURKS AND CAICOS

Turks and Caicos is a great location for shopping lovers, as it offers a range of goods and services that cater to different tastes and budgets. Whether looking for gifts, art, jewellery, fashion, or food, you'll find something to fit your wants and preferences. Here are some of the best places to shop in Turks and Caicos on your trip.

Grace Bay

Grace Bay is Providenciales's main tourist area and also the island's shopping hub. Here you'll find several shopping plazas and gardens that house various shops, stores, galleries, and restaurants. Regent Village, Salt Mills Plaza, and Ports of Call are some of the most famous plazas. You can look through various products, such as local gifts, homemade jewellery, luxury goods, beachwear, makeup, books, and art. Additionally, you may have a meal or a drink at one of the many shops and bars in the area.

Turtle Cove

Turtle Cove is another holiday area in Providenciales that offers some shopping options. Located in central Providenciales, this area has a harbour, several resorts, and a few restaurants and shops. You can find local crafts, gifts, clothes, and items at the shops near the port. Additionally, you may go to the Turks & Caicos National Museum branch at Turtle Cove to learn about the island's history and culture and buy some books or gifts at the museum shop.

Grand Turk Cruise Center

Grand Turk Cruise Center is the main port of call for cruise ships visiting Turks and Caicos. This facility has a big buying area, including duty-free shops, gift stalls, gold stores, clothing outlets, and more. You can find various items here, such as watches, perfumes, leather goods, cigars, rum cakes, conch shells, and t-shirts. You can also enjoy the facilities of the shipping center, such as the swimming pool, the beach, the Margaritaville restaurant and bar, and the FlowRider surf simulator.

TCI Cultural Marketplace

TCI Cultural Marketplace is a one-stop shop for arts, crafts, and gifts in Turks and Caicos. Located on Leeward Highway on Providenciales, this market displays the work of local artists and sellers who sell a range of goods made from natural materials. You can find items such as baskets, hats, bags, mats, toys, paintings, carvings, jewellery, candles, soaps, spices, sauces, jams, and more. You can also enjoy local food and drinks at the market's cafe.

Alverna's Craft Market

Alverna's Craft Market is one of the oldest gift shops in Turks and Caicos. Located on Front Street on Grand Turk, this market sells a range of goods made by local artists and women. You can find conch shells, coral jewellery, wood crafts, drawings, pottery, magnets, keychains, postcards, and more. You can chat with friendly sellers and learn about their stories and skills.

Middle Caicos Co-op

Middle Caicos Co-op is a company that helps more than 40 local artists from Middle Caicos and North Caicos. The co-op sells homemade items that show the island's culture and history. You can find straw baskets, hats, bags, mats, toys, paintings, carvings, jewellery, candles, soaps, spices, sauces, jams, and more. You can also enjoy local food and drinks at the market's cafe.

Jai's Turks and Caicos

Jai's Turks and Caicos is the country's leader in luxury duty-free shopping. With several Providenciales and Grand Turk sites, this shop offers a wide selection of international luxury names, such as Rolex, Cartier, Tiffany, Gucci, Prada, and more. You can find watches, jewellery, cologne, leather items, sunglasses, and accessories at this shop. You can also enjoy careful and individual treatment from the staff.

Graceway Gourmet

Graceway Gourmet is a store that offers a variety of food and beverage items from around the world. Located on Grace Bay Road on Providenciales, this store has a bakery, a cafe, a cheese counter, a salad bar, a sushi bar, and a coffee shop. You can find fresh fruit, organic items, gluten-free goods, veggie choices, wines, beers, drinks, and more. You can also buy ready-made meals or snacks to take away or enjoy at the store's sitting area.

On your trip, these are some of the best places to shop in Turks and Caicos. This part will help you with your trip guide project. Have a wonderful day!

Souvenirs and Gifts

Turks and Caicos is a great place to shop for souvenirs and gifts, whether you want to bring home a piece of the island's culture, nature, or art. The island has a variety of shops that offer unique and locally made goods, from jewellery and clothes to spices and sauces. Whether looking for something for yourself or your loved ones, you'll find plenty of choices to fit your taste and budget. Based on scores, reviews, and demand, here are some of the best items and gifts in Turks and Caicos for 2023-2024.

Jewelry

Turks and Caicos have skilled jewellery makers and artists who create beautiful pieces inspired by the island's colours, shapes, and symbols. You can find jewellery made with silver, gold, sea glass, semi-precious stones, or conch pearls. Some local gold names include Atelys, The Wellington Collection, Jai's Turks and Caicos, Diamonds International Grand Turk, and Serene by Mel.

Fashion

Turks and Caicos have some stylish fashion names that offer clothes and items for men, women, and children. You can find dresses made with silk, cotton, linen, or bamboo, with bright colours and prints reflecting the island's lifestyle.

Some of the local fashion names include Sea Sage, Konk Apparel, Mayaa, and West Indie.

Art

Turks and Caicos have some skilled artists who create paintings, sculptures, pottery, photography, or crafts that showcase the island's beauty, culture, and past. You can find art made with fabric, wood, metal, clay, glass, or shells. Some area art galleries and shops include Anna's Art Gallery, Making Waves Art Studio & Gallery, Paradise Arts Gallery & Gift Shop, The Art Provo Gallery & Boutique, and The Turk's Head Brewery.

Skincare

Turks and Caicos has some natural and organic beauty items that feed and protect your skin from the sun, sand, and salt. You can find grooming items such as soap, lotion, scrub, oil, or sunscreen. Some of the local beauty brands and shops include Wildflower Beauty Lab, Salt Cay Salt Works, Island Organics, and Caribbean Essentials.

Souvenirs

Turks and Caicos have some standard and fun gifts that remind you of your island holiday. You can find facilities such as magnets, keychains, mugs, shot glasses, t-shirts, hats, or bags. Some neighbourhood tourist shops include Mama's Gift Shop, Unicorn Bookstore, Top O' The Cove Deli, Cool Beans Cafe, and Moore Fries.

These are just some of the best items and gifts in Turks and Caicos for 2023-2024, but there are many more to find and enjoy. Whether you want something traditional or trendy, you'll find something to fit your taste and price in this island spot.

Fashion and Accessories

Turks and Caicos is a location for natural beauty, fashion, and items. The islands have a variety of shops and stores that offer clothes, swimwear, jewellery, watches, sunglasses, hats, bags, and more. Whether you're looking for a memory, a gift, or a treat for yourself, you'll find it in Turks and Caicos. Here are some of the best fashion and accessories places in the archipelago, where you can discover the style and quality of this warm location.

Resort Shops

Many Turks and Caicos resorts have shops that sell clothes and items for their guests and tourists. These shops often have a selection of beach and vacation wear and branded clothing and gifts. Some of the best resort shops are The Boutique at Wymara Resort & Villas on Providenciales, which houses the Okaicos swim and lifestyle collection; The Palms Courtyard Shops at The Palms Turks & Caicos on Providenciales, which include an art gallery, a gourmet mini-market, and Wish: a luxurious resort boutique; Coco Boutique at Grace Bay Club on Providenciales, which has a bespoke collection of clothing, swimwear, and accessories; The Landing Bar & Kitchen at Blue Haven Resort & Marina on Providenciales, which has a range of casual and chic clothing and accessories; The Palmetto Boutique at Parrot Cay Resort on Parrot Cay, which has a curated selection of designer clothing, jewelry, and home decor.

Shopping Plazas

If you want to explore more fashion and makeup choices in Turks and Caicos, you can visit some of the buying plazas found on Providenciales. These plazas have a range of locally owned shops that offer fashion and items for different tastes and budgets. Some of the best shopping plazas are The Saltmills Plaza, which has stores such as Blue Surf Shop, Jai's Jewelry Store, Making Waves Art & Events Studio, Panoply Boutique, Paradise Arts Gallery, Unicorn

Bookstore, and West Indies Design; The Regent Village Shopping Center, which has stores such as Anna's Art Gallery & Studio, Atelys Jewelry Design Studio & Gallery, FOTTAC (Flavors of the Turks & Caicos), Graceway Gourmet Market & Deli, Jai's Duty-Free Store & Boutique, Konk Apparel Store & Gallery; The Shops at Grace Bay Plaza, which has stores such as Anna's Too Art Gallery & Studio, Caicos Adventures Dive Shop, Caribbean Outpost, Graceway IGA Supermarket, Island Thyme Gift Shop, Lemon2Go Coffee Shop, Nautique Sports, Ocean Club West Resort Boutique, Potcake Corner Shop, Sea Sage Clothing Store.

Jewelry & Luxury

If you're looking for something more expensive and exclusive in Turks and Caicos, you can find some gold and luxury shops that offer high-end goods and services. These shops often have a range of fine jewellery, watches, sunglasses, cigars, rum, perfume, makeup, and more. Some of the best jewelry and luxury stores are Jai's Jewelry Store & Boutique on Providenciales, which has a collection of diamonds, gold, silver, pearls, and gemstones; Atelys Jewelry Design Studio & Gallery on Providenciales, which has a collection of handmade jewelry inspired by the islands; FOTTAC (Flavors of the Turks & Caicos) on Providenciales, which has a collection of local products such as Bambarra Rum, Turks Head Beer, handcrafted cigars, hot sauce, and spices; The Perfume Bar on Providenciales, which has a collection of fragrances from around the world; The Spa at Grace Bay Club on Providenciales, which has a collection of skincare products from brands such as Natura Bisse, Eminence Organics, and Coola.

Summary

Turks and Caicos is a food lover's dream, with various local and foreign meals and drinks to fit every taste and event. You can enjoy fresh fish, tropical fruits, corn-based basics, and rum-based drinks. You can also find upscale eating, relaxed dining, and street food choices. Whatever you choose, you'll be pleased by the tastes and quality of the food and drink in Turks and Caicos.

CHAPTER 6
OUTDOOR ACTIVITIES IN TURKS AND CAICOS

Turks and Caicos is a paradise for outdoor lovers, as it offers a variety of activities that take advantage of the islands' natural beauty and diversity. Whether you're into water sports, land sports, animals, or excitement, you'll find something to fit your interests and skills. Here are some of the best outdoor things in Turks and Caicos that you should try on your trip.

Snorkeling and Diving

Snorkelling and diving are among the most popular outdoor activities in Turks and Caicos, as the islands boast one of the longest coral reefs in the world and a wealth of marine life. You can swim or dive at many spots around the islands, such as Smith's Reef, Coral Gardens, Malcolm's Road Beach, Northwest Point Marine National Park, Salt Cay Divers, and West Caicos Wall. You'll be amazed by the variety and beauty of the coral formations, sponges, sea fans, and marine animals, such as sharks, rays, turtles, dolphins, and crabs. You can also visit some ships on the ocean floor, such as the Endymion and the H.M.S. Trouvadore.

Kayaking and Paddle Boarding

Kayaking and paddle boarding are great ways to experience the calm and clear waters of Turks and Caicos and the mangrove forests and marshes that provide a vital home for many birds, fish, crabs, and mammals. You can rent a kayak or paddle board from different providers on the islands or join an organized tour that will take you to some of the best places. Some places you can visit by kayak or paddle board are Chalk Sound National Park, Leeward Channel, Mangrove Cay, Iguana Island, Bottle Creek Lagoon, and Three Mary Cays.

Whale Watching

Whale watching is an exciting sport that will allow you to see humpback whales in their natural surroundings. Every year, from January to April, thousands of these beautiful creatures pass through the seas of Turks and Caicos to their breeding grounds in the Dominican Republic. You can take a whale-watching tour to get close to these gentle giants or even swim or dive with them if you're lucky. You'll be amazed by their size, ease, and songs as they interact.

Hiking and Biking

Hiking and biking are excellent activities to enjoy the beautiful scenery and wildlife of Turks and Caicos. You can hike or bike on various trails on the islands, such as Crossing Place Trail on Middle Caicos, Conch Bar Caves Trail on Middle Caicos, North Creek Trail on Grand Turk, Cheshire Hall Plantation Trail on Providenciales, Long Bay Beach Trail on Providenciales, and Blue Hills Road Trail on Providenciales. You'll see beautiful views of the beaches, hills, caves, farms, marshes, and wildlife along the way.

Horseback Riding

Horseback riding is a fun and romantic activity that will let you experience the beauty of Turks and Caicos from a different view. You can ride a horse along some of the most beautiful beaches in the world, such as Grace Bay Beach, Long Bay Beach, or Sapodilla Bay Beach. You can also ride a horse through the paths and hills of Long Bay Hills, where you'll see local plants and birds. You can book a horseback riding tour with one of the operators on the island, such as Provo Ponies, Unique Tours and Rentals, or Heritage Tours and Horseback Riding.

Golfing

Golfing is another outdoor sport you can enjoy in Turks and Caicos, as the islands have a world-class golf course that caters to all players. The Provo Golf Club is an 18-hole championship course on Providenciales, near Grace Bay. The system boasts green fields, difficult traps, water dangers, and beautiful views of the ocean and the marshes. You can also practice your swing at the driving range, putting green, or chipping area. The club also has a pro shop, a diner, and a bar.

Kiteboarding

Kiteboarding is an exciting sport that mixes surfing, sailing, and flying. You can slide across the water on a board while being pulled by a kite that uses wind power. Turks and Caicos is one of the best places to kiteboard in the Caribbean, as it has steady trade winds, warm water, and small bays. The best spot to kiteboard is Long Bay Beach on Providenciales, where you'll find flat water and a steady breeze. You can rent tools or take lessons from one of the kiteboarding schools on the island, such as Kite Provo, Big Blue Collective, or TC Kiteboarding.

These are some of the best outdoor things in Turks and Caicos that you can try on your trip.

Parks and Gardens

Turks and Caicos is a paradise for nature lovers, with its stunning beaches, blue waves, and diverse marine life. But the island also has some beautiful parks and gardens that offer a different view of the island's scenery, plants, and wildlife. Whether you want to relax, explore, or learn, you'll find plenty of choices to enjoy the green areas of Turks and Caicos. Based on scores, reviews, and popularity, here are some of the best parks and gardens in Turks and Caicos for 2023-2024.

Chalk Sound National Park

Chalk Sound National Park is a natural lake with hundreds of small rocky rocks and crystal-clear water. The park is situated in the southwest of Providenciales and covers an area of about 5 square miles (13 square kilometres). The park is great for enjoying the views, kayaking, paddleboard, or swimming. You can also visit the nearby Sapodilla Bay Beach or Taylor Bay Beach for rest.

Location: Providenciales

Website: https://www.visittci.com/providenciales/chalk-sound-national-park

Princess Alexandra National Park

Princess Alexandra National Park is a marine park that includes part of the north coast of Providenciales, including the popular Grace Bay Beach. The park covers an area of about 15 square miles (39 square kilometres) and protects a range of ecosystems, such as coral reefs, seagrass beds, mangroves, and marshes. The park is a great place to enjoy the beach, swim, dive, or spot wildlife like turtles, dolphins, rays, or birds.

Location: Providenciales
Website

Columbus Landfall National Park

Columbus Landfall National Park is a marine park that covers the west coast of Grand Turk, including the famous Cockburn Town. The park covers an area of about 6 square miles (16 square kilometres) and protects a range of environments, such as coral reefs, seagrass beds, mangroves, and salt ponds. The park is a great place to enjoy history, swim, dive, or spot wildlife like whales, sharks, turtles, or birds.

Location: Grand Turk

Website: https://www.visittci.com/grand-turk/columbus-landfall-national-park

Bajari Garden

Bajari Garden is a natural garden with a mix of local and foreign plants worldwide. The garden is situated in the south of Providenciales and covers an area of about 2 acres (0.8 hectares). The yard is a great place to enjoy the plants' colours, scents, and forms, as well as learn about their uses and benefits. You can also visit the nearby Cheshire Hall Plantation for some history.

Location: Providenciales

Turks and Caicos National Museum Botanical and Cultural Garden

Turks and Caicos National Museum Botanical and Cultural Garden is a botanical and cultural garden that features a collection of local and historical plants, displays, and items connected to the island's history and culture. The park is north of Grand Turk, next to the Turks and Caicos National Museum. The park is a great place to enjoy the island's beauty, variety, and tradition and learn about its nature and human past.

Location: Grand Turk

Website: https://www.tcmuseum.org

Turks Head Brewery Garden

Turks Head Brewery Garden is a beer garden with a collection of tropical plants, a brewery, and a bar. The park is east of Providenciales, next to the Turks Head Brewery. The park is great for enjoying the scenery, tasting the local beer, or taking a brewery tour.

Location: Providenciales

These are just some of the best parks and gardens in Turks and Caicos for 2023-2024, but there are many more to find and enjoy. Whether you want to relax, explore, or learn, you'll find something to fit your interest and mood in this island spot.

Archipelago cruise

Turks and Caicos is a group of 40 islands and cays inhabited by nine. Each island has its beauty, character, and sights and offers a different view of this beautiful place. If you want to explore more than one island during your stay, you can plan an archipelago trip that will take you to some of the most amazing places in Turks and Caicos. Here are some of the best ways to enjoy an island trip in Turks and Caicos, including where to go, what to do, and how to get there.

Providenciales

Providenciales, also known as Provo, is the main tourist island in Turks and Caicos and the entrance to the rest of the group. It is home to the beautiful Grace Bay Beach, which TripAdvisor named the best beach in the world. It also has a range of upscale resorts, restaurants, shops, spas, golf courses, and nightlife places. Providenciales is the best base for your archipelago trip, as it has the most plane and boat links to other islands. You can easily spend a few days in Provo, enjoying its sights and services, before heading out to other islands.

Grand Turk

Grand Turk is the capital island of Turks and Caicos and the political and cultural hub of the country. You can find government offices, the National Museum, the Grand Turk Lighthouse, and many historical buildings. Grand Turk is also known for its great diving and swimming spots, such as the Grand Turk Wall, which drops to over 7,000 feet (2,134 meters). Grand Turk has a relaxed and laid-back vibe, with friendly locals and lovely shops. You can get to Grand Turk from Providenciales by a 25-minute flight or a 90-minute boat ride.

Grand Turk https://www.visittci.com/grand-turk

Salt Cay

Salt Cay is a small and private island that gives a glimpse into the past of Turks and Caicos. It was once a major source of salt in the Caribbean and still has many salt ponds and windmills that date back to the 17th century. Salt Cay is also a great place to see humpback whales during their yearly passage from January to April. You can watch them from the shore or take a whale-watching tour. Salt Cay has a few guest houses, bars, and shops but no casinos or nightlife. You can get to Salt Cay from Grand Turk by a 15-minute flight or a 30-minute boat ride.

[Salt Cay](https://www.visittci.com/salt-cay

South Caicos

South Caicos is the fishing capital of Turks and Caicos and the source of most of the seafood served in the country. It has a big natural harbour, where you can see bright fishing boats and local fishermen at work. South Caicos has some of the most beautiful beaches and islands in Turks and Caicos, such as Long Beach, Plandon Cay Cut, and Sail Rock. South Caicos has a few upscale resorts, such as Sailrock Resort and East Bay Resort, as well as some local guest houses and restaurants. You can get to South Caicos from Providenciales by a 25-minute flight or a 90-minute boat ride.

South Caicos

Middle Caicos

Middle Caicos is the biggest island in Turks and Caicos but also one of the least crowded. It has some of the most beautiful natural sites in the country, such as Mudjin

Harbour, Bambarra Beach, Conch Bar Caves, and Crossing Place Trail. Middle Caicos also has some of the most true cultural events in Turks and Caicos, such as basket spinning, model ship making, and yearly gatherings. Middle Caicos has a few houses, huts, and hotels but no clubs or nightlife. You can get to Middle Caicos from Providenciales by a 25-minute flight to North Caicos and a 30-minute drive across a channel.

Winter activities

Turks and Caicos is a dream spot for winter vacation, with warm weather, open skies, and blue seas. The islands offer a range of activities for every interest and skill level, from relaxing on the beach to exploring the underground world.

Here are some of the best winter sports in Turks and Caicos.

Snorkeling and Diving

Turks and Caicos have some of the best fishing and diving places in the Caribbean, with clear water, beautiful coral reefs, and rich marine life. You can swim or dive all year round, but winter is especially good for finding whales, dolphins, rays, and turtles. You can choose from places such as Grace Bay, Bight Reef, Smith's Reef, Northwest Point, West Caicos, French Cay, or Salt Cay. You can also join a boat tour or a private cruise to take you to the best spots. Caicos Dream Tours, Island Vibes Tours, and Big Blue Collective are some of the best swimming and diving companies.

Sailing and Cruising

Sailing and touring are great ways to enjoy the views and the breeze of Turks and Caicos. You can sail along the coast of Providenciales, visit the empty cays and islands, or watch the sunset over the ocean. You can also take a glow worm walk showing you the bioluminescent worms that light up the water after the full moon. You can choose from different types of boats, such as catamarans, yachts, or powerboats, based on your taste and price. Some of the best sailing and touring companies are TCI Safari Tours, Sand & Sea Tours, and Sail Beluga.

Fishing

Fishing is a popular sport in Turks and Caicos, with a range of fish to catch and eat. Based on your skill level and taste, you can fish inshore or offshore. Inshore fishing is good for bonefish, tarpon, snook, barracuda, jacks, snapper, grouper, and more. Offshore fishing is good for tuna, wahoo, mahi-mahi, marlin, sailfish, swordfish, and more. You can also join a bottom fishing or reef fishing tour that will take you to the best spots for getting crab, lobster, or other seafood. Panoply Sport Fishing & Luxury Charters, Grand Slam Fishing Charters, and Catchin' Caicos are some of the best fishing companies.

Shopping

Shopping is a fun way to spend a winter day in Turks and Caicos. You can find a range of gifts, crafts, art, jewelry, clothes, spices, rum cakes, sauces, and more. You can shop at the local markets, such as Thursday Fish Fry or Saltmills Plaza Market Day, at the expensive stores at Regent Village or Ports of Call, or the unique shops at Blue Hills Road or Leeward Highway. Some of the best places to shop are Anna's Art Gallery, Mama's Gift Shop, FOTTAC (Flavors Of The Turks And Caicos), Turk's Head Brewery, Bambarra Rum Company, or The Wellington Collection.

Summary

Turks and Caicos is a winter wonderland for tourists who love the sun, sea, and sand. The islands have various things for every taste and price, from swimming and diving to sailing and exploring to kayaking and paddleboarding to fishing and shopping. Whatever you choose, you'll have an amazing time in Turks and Caicos.

CHAPTER 7

SURROUNDING AREAS OF TURKS AND CAICOS

Turks and Caicos is a British Overseas Territory that consists of 40 islands and cays in the Caribbean. The islands are surrounded by other countries and regions that offer different sights and experiences for tourists. Whether you want to explore more of the Bahamas, visit the Dominican Republic, or discover Cuba, you'll find something to fit your interests and budget. Here are some surrounding places of Turks and Caicos that you can visit on your trip.

The Bahamas

The Bahamas is a country that comprises more than 700 islands, cays, and islets in the Atlantic Ocean. The Bahamas is the closest friend of Turks and Caicos, as they share the same island and ocean border. The Bahamas is known for its beautiful beaches, coral reefs, wildlife, culture, and history. You can visit some of the most famous islands in the Bahamas, such as Nassau, Paradise Island, Grand Bahama, Abaco, Eleuthera, Exuma, Andros, Bimini, and San Salvador. You can also discover some of the less-visited islands, such as Cat Island, Long Island, Inagua, Acklins,

Crooked Island, Mayaguana, and Ragged Island. You can travel to the Bahamas by plane or boat from Turks and Caicos.

Dominican Republic

The Dominican Republic is a country that covers the eastern two-thirds of the island of Hispaniola in the Caribbean Sea. The Dominican Republic is the second nearest friend of Turks and Caicos, as they are divided by about 100 miles (160 km) of water. The Dominican Republic is known for its varied scenery, rich culture, lively music, delicious food, and friendly people.

You can visit some of the most famous places in the Dominican Republic, such as Santo Domingo, Punta Cana, Puerto Plata, Samana, La Romana, Santiago, Jarabacoa, and Barahona. You can also discover some of the less-known places, such as Pedernales, Monte Cristi, Constanza, Bayahibe, Las Terrenas, and Cabarete. You can fly to the Dominican Republic by plane from Turks and Caicos.

Cuba

Cuba is a country that consists of the island of Cuba and several smaller islands in the Caribbean Sea. Cuba is the third closest friend of Turks and Caicos, as they are divided by about 150 miles (240 km) of water. Cuba is known for its revolutionary past, communist system, colonial building, classic cars, cigars, rum, music, dance, and art. You can visit some of the most famous places in Cuba, such as Havana, Varadero, Cienfuegos, Santiago de Cuba, Viñales, Trinidad, and Baracoa. You can also visit less-known places, such as Camagüey, Holguín, Matanzas, Remedios, and Gibara. You can travel to Cuba by plane or boat from Turks and Caicos.

Haiti

Haiti is a country that covers the western third of the island of Hispaniola in the Caribbean Sea. Haiti is the fourth closest neighbor of Turks and Caicos, divided by about 200 miles (320 km) of water. Haiti is known for its rich and complicated culture, history, art, music, and faith. You can visit some of the most famous places in Haiti, such as Port-au-Prince, Cap-Haïtien, Jacmel, Labadee, and Île-à-Vache. You can also discover less-known places like Les Cayes, Hinche, Milot, and Bassin-Bleu. You can fly to Haiti by plane from Turks and Caicos.

To conclude, Turks and Caicos is a beautiful and diverse location that offers many sights and activities for tourists.

However, if you want to explore more of the Caribbean area, you can also visit some of the nearby countries and regions that have their charm and attraction. Whether you stay in Turks and Caicos or travel to nearby areas, you'll have a unique and enjoyable trip.

CHAPTER 8

7-DAY ITINERARY IN TURKS AND CAICOS

Turks and Caicos is a beautiful Caribbean location that offers visitors a wide range of activities and sites. From sitting on the clean beaches and swimming in the blue waters to studying the history and culture of the islands and trying the

local food, there is something for everyone in this island paradise. This 7-day schedule will show you how to make the most of your time in Turks and Caicos, covering the best of what the islands have to offer.

Day 1: Arrive in Providenciales and Relax on Grace Bay Beach

On your first day, you will arrive in Providenciales, the main island and entrance to Turks and Caicos. You can take a cab or a bus from the airport to your hotel or resort, which will likely be located on or near Grace Bay Beach, one of the most beautiful beaches in the world. After checking in, you can spend the rest of the day resting on the soft white sand, swimming in the clear blue water, or enjoying your accommodation services. You can also walk along the beach and check out some nearby shops, restaurants, and bars.

Location: Providenciales

Day 2: Snorkel at Smith's Reef and Kayak at Chalk Sound

On your second day, you will discover some of the natural wonders of Providenciales. In the morning, you will head to Smith's Reef, one of the best diving places on the island. You can rent diving gear from a local shop, bring your own and then enter the water from the beach. You will be surprised by the beautiful coral reefs and various marine life that you will see, such as fish, turtles, rays, and even sharks. You can also spot some ships and underwater art along the way.

In the afternoon, you will head to Chalk Sound National Park, a natural bay with hundreds of small rocky islands and crystal-clear water. You can rent a kayak or a paddle board from a local company or bring your own and then explore the
lake at your own pace. You will enjoy the views, calm, and wildlife you will meet, such as iguanas, birds, and fish. You

can also visit the nearby Sapodilla Bay Beach or Taylor Bay Beach for some rest.

Location: Providenciales

Day 3: Visit Iguana Island and Adopt a Potcake

On your third day, you will visit another island and meet some animal friends. In the morning, you will take a boat or kayak tour to Iguana Island, also known as Little Water Cay. This island is home to hundreds of rare rock iguanas that walk freely. You can walk along the boardwalks and watch these interesting critters up close. You can also enjoy some diving or swimming around the island.

In the afternoon, you will head back to Providenciales and visit Potcake Place, a dog rescue group that helps homeless dogs find loving homes. Potcakes are a mixed breed of dogs native to Turks and Caicos and other Caribbean islands.
They are named after the extra food that people used to give them. You can offer to take a pot cake for a walk on the beach, play with them, or even adopt one if you fall in love with them.

Location: Providenciales and Little Water Cay

Day 4: ATV Tour and Catch Your Own Conch for Dinner

On your fourth day, you will have some fun and excitement on land and sea. In the morning, you will join an ATV tour that will take you around the island and show you some of its hidden gems. You will ride along dirt roads, trails, and beaches and see some of the island's highlights, such as the Conch Farm, the Blue Hills, the Cheshire Hall Plantation, and the Hole. You will also enjoy some beautiful views and picture chances along the way.

In the afternoon, you will join a boat tour that will take you to a conch farm, where you will learn how to catch and clean your own conch. Conch is a type of shellfish that is a treat in Turks and Caicos and other Caribbean islands. You will also enjoy some diving or swimming around the farm. You will then head to a nearby beach, making and eating your fresh conch salad, along with some other local foods and drinks.

Location: Providenciales

Day 5: Beach Hop

On your fifth day, you will enjoy some of the best beaches in Turks and Caicos. You can rent a car or a scooter, take a cab or a shuttle, and visit some of the island's most beautiful and famous sites. You can spend as much time as you want on each beach, based on your mood and taste. Here are some of the places that you can visit:

Grace Bay Beach: This is the most popular beach in Turks and Caicos and for good reason. It has soft white sand, clear blue water, and plenty of facilities like hotels, restaurants, shops, and bars. It is also great for fishing, swimming, or sunbathing.

Long Bay Beach: This beach is great for kite surfing, with steady winds and flat water. It is also great for resting, as it is less busy and more private than Grace Bay Beach. It has soft white sand, blue water, and palm trees.

Leeward Beach: This is a great beach for walks, as it has a long stretch of sand that links to Grace Bay Beach. It is also great for swimming, with calm water and no rocks or seaweed. It has soft white sand, clear blue water, and shade from trees.

Pelican Beach: This is a great beach for diving, as it has a coral reef close to the shore. It is also great for resting, as it is quiet and peaceful. It has soft white sand, blue water, and rocks and shells.

Location: Providenciales

Day 6: Trip to Salt Cay On your sixth day

you will visit another island and experience its history and beauty. You will take a flight or a boat from Providenciales to Salt Cay, a small and rustic island that was once the center of the salt business in Turks and Caicos. You will spend the day touring the island and its highlights, such as:

The Salt House: This museum shows the history and culture of Salt Cay and its salt business. You will see displays, objects, and pictures that tell the story of the island and its people.

The White House: This is a unique house that was once the home of the salt commissioner. You will see the building, furniture, and art that show the colonial age of the island.

The Salinas: These are the salt ponds used to make seawater salt. You will seen the remains of the windmills, pumps, ditches, and walls that were used to run the salt business.

The Beaches: Salt Cay has some beautiful, isolated beaches that are great for resting, swimming, or fishing. You can visit some beaches like North Beach, South Beach, or Balfour Town Beach.

Location: Salt Cay

Day 7: Explore the History of Turks and Caicos

Before Departing On your last day, you will discover some of the history and culture of Turks and Caicos before leaving. You will visit some of the island's important places and museums, such as:

The Turks and Caicos National Museum: This museum shows the nature and human past of Turks and Caicos. You will see displays, objects, and pictures that tell the story of the island's geology, environment, history, enslaved people, pirates, shipwrecks, and more.

- **The Grand Turk Lighthouse:** This famous lighthouse was built in 1852 to guide ships around the reef. You will see the lighthouse, its keeper's house, and its grounds. Additionally, you will appreciate some lovely vistas of the island.

- **Her Majesty's Jail:** This famous jail was built in 1830 to house thieves and inmates. You will see the jail cells, the gallows, and the exhibits that tell the story of the prison's past and prisoners.

After visiting these places, you will return to Providenciales and catch your flight or boat. You will leave with amazing memories and adventures from your 7-day schedule in Turks and Caicos.

Location: Grand Turk
Website: https://www.tcmuseum.org

To conclude, Turks and Caicos is a great location for a 7-day plan that includes rest and excitement. You can enjoy the stunning beaches, the turquoise waters, and the diverse marine life, as well as explore the history and culture of the islands and taste the local food. Turks and Caicos is worth visiting for its beauty, variety, and charm.

CHAPTER 9
PRACTICAL INFORMATION AND TIPS FOR TURKS AND CAICOS

Etiquette and customs

Turks and Caicos is a nice and welcoming place where you can enjoy the kindness and culture of the local people. However, as with any country, there are some manners and practices that you should be aware of and follow during your stay. Here are some essential techniques and practises in Turks and Caicos, including how to meet, dress, tip, and behave.

Greeting

The people in Turks and Caicos are very kind and polite and believe in having good

manners and exercising respect. When meeting someone for the first time, a handshake is the normal form of welcome, followed by a friendly saying such as

"Hello", "Good morning", or "Good afternoon". If you are presented to someone older or more senior than you, you should call them by their title and surname, such as "Mr Smith" or "Dr Jones", unless they ask you to use their first name. If you are meeting someone you already know, a hug or a kiss on the cheek may be acceptable based on the amount of comfort and friendship. Eye contact is also important, as it shows interest and truthfulness.

Dressing

Turks and Caicos are warm, so light and casual clothes are ideal for most events. Shorts, T-shirts, shoes, sunglasses, and sun hats are popular clothing for both men and women during the day, especially on the beach or in town. However, some companies, such as stores, banks, or government offices, have limits on beachwear being allowed clothing for entry. In these cases, you should cover up with a shirt or a dress and wear shoes. Public nudity is also banned in Turks and Caicos, so you should not go topless or wear thongs on the beach. In the evening, especially in winter, you may need a light sweater or jacket, as it can get cooler after sunset. Most places have a casual dress code, but some may require more formal clothing, such as buttoned shirts or long pants for men or dresses or skirts for women. You should check with the place before you go or ask your hotel staff for help.

Tipping

Tipping is required for most service jobs in Turks and Caicos, such as cab drivers, waitpersons, bartenders, tour guides, housekeepers, pool workers, etc. The normal tip is around 15% of the bill or fare unless a service charge is included. Some tourism-oriented companies charge a service charge of 10% to 15%, which is similar to a tip or gratuity, but is different in that all non-managerial workers of the business share it. You can check your bill or ticket to see if a service charge is added or ask the staff if you need more clarificationIf there is no service charge, leave a tip in cash or add it to your credit card payment. You can also tip more if you are very happy with the service.

Behaviour

Turks and Caicos is a relatively safe and quiet place, but there are some basic rules of behavior that you should follow to avoid any trouble or offence. You should follow the country's laws, society, faith, and surroundings and avoid rude acts. Some of the methods to avoid are:

- Littering, harming, or destroying any natural or historical places.

- Harassing, upsetting, or feeding any wildlife or sea life.
- Taking any coral, shells, or plants from the beach or the sea without permission.
- Making excessive noise, especially at night or near private areas.
- Engaging in any public shows of love that may be considered indecent or improper.
- Discussing any sensitive or controversial topics, such as politics or religion, that may cause fights or differences.

By following these rules, you will show your respect and admiration for the people and the country and enjoy their kindness and culture. Have a great time in Turks and Caicos!

Language and communication

Turks and Caicos is a varied and international location where you can hear different languages and accents. The islands have a rich and complicated past, affected by the native Taíno, African, European, and Caribbean societies. Here are some tips and knowledge on language and conversation in Turks and Caicos.

Official Language

The official language of Turks and Caicos is English, as the islands are a British Overseas Territory. English is used in business, school, culture, and tourists. You'll be fine speaking English with the people, staff, or other tourists.

However, you may notice differences in speech, spelling, and grammar, as Turks and Caicos English is affected by British, American, and Caribbean English.

Creole Language

The most popular second language in Turks and Caicos is Creole, also called Turks and Caicos Creole or Belonger Creole. Creole is a language that emerged from the touch between English and African languages during the colonial era. Many of the local islands, called Belongers, speak

Creole. Creole has its language, vocabulary, and phrases but shares some words with English. You may hear some Creole terms or comments when you meet with the people, such as:

- Mèsi: Thank you
- Tanpri: Please
- Bon jour: Good day
- Bon swé: Good night
- What da Wybe?: What's up?
- I straight: It's all good
- Een nothin: Nothing much
- Axe: Ask

Other Languages

Turks and Caicos is home to people from over 60 countries, so you may also hear other languages on the islands. Some of the most popular ones are Spanish, French, Italian, Haitian Creole, and Portuguese. Spanish is especially common, as many newcomers from Cuba, Dominican Republic, Puerto Rico, and other Latin American countries exist. You may also find some signs or tables in Spanish or French in some places.

Communication Tips

Turks and Caicos is a nice and inviting location where you can easily connect with the locals and the tourists. Here are some tips to make your conversation easier and more enjoyable:

- Greet people with a smile and a kiss. You can also say "Good day" or "Good evening" based on the time of day.
- Be nice and thoughtful. Use "please", "thank you", "excuse me", and "sorry" when suitable.
- Be aware of societal differences. Turks and Caicos have a mix of British, American, Caribbean, and African cultures, so that you may meet different habits, values, or beliefs. Try to be open-minded and interested.

- Ask for help if you need it. Turks and Caicos people are usually helpful and friendly. If you have any questions or problems, feel free to ask someone for help or advice.

- Have fun and enjoy the talk. Turks and Caicos people are warm and friendly. They like to chat, joke, laugh, and share stories. Be bold to join in or start a chat.

Summary

Turks and Caicos is an interesting place to experience different languages and countries. The main language is English, but you may also hear Creole or other languages spoken by locals or newcomers. You can talk easily with anyone on the islands by following simple tips and etiquette. You'll also have a great time learning more about the past and society of Turks and Caicos through language and conversation.

Simple words and terms to know

Turks and Caicos is a British Overseas Territory with English as its legal language. However, you may also meet some versions of English spoken by different groups of people on the islands, such as Turks and Caicos Creole, Jamaican Patois, or Haitian Creole. Knowing some easy words and terms in these languages can help you better interact with people and understand their society. Here are some simple words and phrases to know in Turks and Caicos.

Turks and Caicos Creole

Turks and Caicos Creole is a form of English affected by African languages. It is spoken by many people on the islands, especially on Grand Turk, Salt Cay, South Caicos, and Middle Caicos. Some of the features of Turks and Caicos Creole are:

- The use of "me" instead of "I" or "my", such as"me name" (my name) or "me hungry" (I'm hungry).
- The use of "dem" instead of "them" or "they", such as "dem people" (those people) or "dem gone" (they left).

- The use of "a" instead of "is" or "are", such as "she a teacher" (she is a teacher) or "we a happy" (we are happy).
- The use of double negatives, such as "me no see nothing" (I didn't see anything) or "me no like nobody" (I don't like anyone).
- The use of "an" instead of "and", such as "me a you" (me and you) or "fish a chips" (fish and chips).

Some popular words and sentences in Turks and Caicos Creole are:

- Hello: Hello
- Goodbye: Bye-bye
- Thank you: Tank you
- Please: Please
- Yes: Yeah
- No: No
- How are you?: How you do?
- I'm fine: Me good
- What is your name?: What you name?
- My name is...: Me name...
- Where are you from?: Where you from?
- I'm from...: Me from...

- How much is this?: How much dis?
- Do you speak English?: You speak English?
- I don't understand: Me no understand
- Excuse me: Excuse me
- Sorry: Sorry
- Cheers: Cheers
- Enjoy your meal: Enjoy you food
- Have a nice day: Have a nice day

Jamaican Patois

Jamaican Patois is a form of English inspired by Spanish and French. It is spoken by some people on the islands, especially on Providenciales, where many Jamaicans live and work. Some of the features of Jamaican Patois are:

- The use of "mi" instead of "I" or "my", such as"mi name" (my name) or "mi hungry" (I'm hungry).
- The use of "dem" instead of "them" or "they", such as "dem people" (those people) or "dem gone" (they left).
- The use of "a" instead of "is" or "are", such as "she a teacher" (she is a teacher) or "we a happy" (we are happy).

- The use of double negatives, such as "mi no see nutten" (I didn't see anything) or "mi no like nobody" (I don't like anyone).
- The use of "an'" instead of "and", such as "mi an'you" (me and you) or "fish an' chips" (fish and chips).

Some popular words and sentences in Jamaican Patois are:

- Hello: Hello
- Goodbye: Lata
- Thank you: Tank yuh
- Please: Please
- Yes: Yes
- No: No
- How are you?: How yuh stay?
- I'm fine: Mi good
- What is your name?: Wah yuh name?
- My name is...: Mi name...
- Where are you from?: Weh yuh from?
- I'm from...: Mi from...
- How much is this?: How much fi dis?
- Do you speak English?: Yuh speak English?
- I don't understand: Mi no undastan'

- Excuse me: Eskize mwen
- Sorry: Padon
- Cheers: Tchè
- Enjoy your meal: Bon apeti
- Have a nice day: Pase yon bèl jounen
- Have a good journey: Bon vwayaj

Theseare some simple words and terms to know in Turks and Caicos. Learning these phrases can help you better interact with the locals and understand their culture. However, you can handle the language problem, as most island people can speak or understand English. Have fun, and enjoy your trip!

Health and Safety Tips in Turks and Caicos

Turks and Caicos is a great location for tourists who want to enjoy the Caribbean's beauty, culture, and excitement. The islands are known for their beautiful beaches, blue seas, and diverse marine life. However, like any other place, Turks and Caicos also have health and safety risks that visitors should be aware of and prepared for. Here are some health and safety tips in Turks and Caicos for 2023-2024, based on the latest information and suggestions.

Health Tips

- Turks and Caicos have no major health risks or illnesses, such as malaria, yellow fever, or Zika virus. However, visitors should still consult their doctor before going and make sure they are up to date with their regular vaccines, such as measles, mumps, rubella, tetanus, diphtheria, polio, hepatitis A, and hepatitis B.

- Travelers should also consider getting vaccines for typhoid and rabies, especially if they plan to visit country places or contact animals. Travelers should also bring their stock of prescription medications and over-the-counter medicines for common illnesses, such as painkillers, antihistamines, antidiarrheals, and rehydration salts.

- Travelers should avoid drinking tap water or ice made from tap water in Turks and Caicos, as it may be contaminated with germs or bugs. Travelers should drink bottled water or boiled water instead. Travelers should also avoid eating raw or undercooked food, especially fish, meat, eggs, and dairy products. Travelers should wash their hands frequently with soap and water or use alcohol-based hand sanitizer to prevent the spread of germs.

- Travelers should protect themselves from the sun and heat in Turks and Caicos, as they can cause sunburn, dehydration, heat stroke, or heat exhaustion. Travelers should wear sunscreen with SPF 30 or higher, sunglasses, a hat, and a cover-up. Travelers should also drink plenty of water and avoid alcohol and coffee. Travelers should seek shade or air-conditioning during the hottest hours of the day and avoid hard activities.

- Travelers should protect themselves from bug bites in Turks and Caicos, as they can cause itchiness, swelling, allergic responses, or infections. Travelers should wear long-sleeved shirts, long pants, socks, and shoes. Travelers should also use bug protection with DEET or picaridin on uncovered skin and clothes. Travelers should also sleep under a mosquito net or in an air-conditioned room with protected windows and doors.

- Travelers should be careful when swimming or diving in Turks and Caicos, as they can meet dangerous sea animals or currents. Travelers should swim only in marked places with lifeguards or guides. Travelers should also wear protective clothing or equipment, such as rash guards, wetsuits, fins, nets, and snorkels. Travelers should also avoid touching or eating any sea animals, such as coral, fish, stingrays, or sharks. Travelers should also avoid swimming alone, at night, or after drinking.

Safety Tips

- Turks and Caicos is usually safe and peaceful, with a low crime rate and a nice community. However, visitors should still practise care and common sense, as they can face minor crimes, such as theft, pickpocketing, or scams. Travelers should also be aware of the chance of violent crimes, such as robbery and attack, especially in deserted or dark areas or at night.

- Avoid carrying large amounts of cash or items, such as gold, electronics, or IDs. Travelers should also use a hotel safe or a box to store their goods. Travelers should also make copies of their important papers, such as IDs, visas, tickets, and insurance cards. Travelers should also keep their things close to them and never leave them unattended.

- Avoid going alone or in unknown places, especially at night. Travelers should also avoid taking paths or alleys. Travelers should also use reliable taxis or rental cars to get around the island. Travelers should also avoid hitching or accepting rides from strangers.

Travelers should also be aware of their surroundings and trust their senses.

- Avoid getting involved in disagreements or fights with locals or other tourists. Travelers should also follow the local rules, traditions, and society. Travelers should also avoid any political rallies or riots.

- Travelers should register with their office or consulate before going to Turks and Caicos. Travelers should also have the contact information of their office or consulate in case of an emergency. Travelers should also have the contact information of a nearby doctor or hospital in case of an illness or accident.

Conclusion

Turks and Caicos is a beautiful and safe location for tourists who want to enjoy the Caribbean. However, tourists should still follow some health and safety tips to ensure a smooth and enjoyable trip. By being prepared and careful, tourists can have a pleasant and trouble-free holiday in Turks and Caicos.

Emergency contacts

Turks and Caicos is a generally safe and quiet place, but in case of any problem, you should know who to call and how to get help. Here are some of the key emergency sources in Turks and Caicos, including the police, fire, ambulance, hospital, crisis management, and diplomatic services.

Police, Fire, and Ambulance

The emergency line for police, fire, and medical in Turks and Caicos is 911. You can call this number from any home or cell phone, free of charge. You should provide your name, address, and the nature of the situation. The operator will send the right service to your address immediately. You should stay cool and follow the operator's advice until help comes.

Hospital

Turks and Caicos has two state hospitals: Cheshire Hall Medical Centre in Providenciales and Cockburn Town Medical Centre in Grand Turk. Both hospitals have 24-hour emergency rooms that can handle most medical situations. They also have hospital rooms, outpatient centres, testing, drug, and expert services. InterHealth Canada, a Canadian healthcare company, operates the hospitals. You can call the doctors at:

- Cheshire Hall Medical Centre: +1 (649) 941-2800
- Cockburn Town Medical Centre: +1 (649) 946-1000

InterHealth Canada

Disaster Management

Turks and Caicos has a Department of Disaster Management and Emergencies (DDME) responsible for managing the reaction to natural or man-made disasters, such as storms,
earthquakes, floods, fires, or accidents. The DDME also offers knowledge and help on disaster preparation, prevention, healing, and resilience. You can reach the DDME at:

- Providenciales: +1 (649) 338-4039
- Grand Turk: +1 (649) 338-3672

- North Caicos: +1 (649) 338-6401

- Middle Caicos: +1 (649) 331-8670
- Salt Cay: +1 (649) 338-6981 - South Caicos: +1 (649) 946-3211

DDME

Consular Services

Turks and Caicos is a British Overseas Territory, which means it is under the authority of the United Kingdom but has its government and laws. If you are a British citizen or a member of another Commonwealth country, you can call the British High Commission in Nassau, Bahamas, for legal help in Turks and Caicos. The High Commission can help you with problems such as documents, visas, travel information, law concerns, emergencies, or return. You can reach the High Commission at:

Phone: +1 (242) 225-6033
Email: UKinBahamas@fco.gov.uk
Website: https://www.gov.uk/world/organisations/british-high-commission-nassau

If you are a citizen of another country, you can call your local office or consulate for legal help in Turks and Caicos.

Some countries have special consuls or officials in Turks and Caicos, such as Canada, France, Germany, Italy, the Netherlands, and the United States. You can find their personal information on their individual websites or on the Turks and Caicos government

These are some of the key emergency links in Turks and Caicos that will help you get help and support in any emergency. You should keep these contacts handy and available during your visit. Before you journey, you should also check the latest travel advice and tips from your government or office. Have a safe and fun trip to Turks and Caicos!

Communication and Internet Access

Turks and Caicos is a modern and linked location where you can quickly interact and access the internet. The islands have a stable and fast internet network with two local providers: Flow and Digicel. You can use your own phone, buy a local

SIM card, or rent a phone or hotspot. You can also find free Wi-Fi in many places or use cellphone internet. Here are some of the best tips and information on contact and internet connection in Turks and Caicos.

Phone

You can use your phone in Turks and Caicos if it suits the local network and is open. Turks and Caicos uses GSM 850/1900 MHz for 2G/3G/4G and CDMA 800 MHz for 2G/3G. You can check your phone's connectivity here: https://willmyphonework.net/

You'll also need to set up foreign roaming with your service before you leave or buy a roaming plan if offered. However, traveling can be expensive, so consider other choices.

You can buy a local SIM card from Flow or Digicel, giving you a local number and access to cheaper rates for calls, texts, and the internet. You'll need an unlocked GSM phone to use a local SIM card. You can buy a SIM card at the airport or any of the provider's shops or agents on the islands. You'll need to show an ID to register your SIM card. You can also buy prepaid credit or plans for your SIM card at different places.

You can rent a phone or a hotspot from local companies such as Islandcom Wireless, Cellhire, or TravelCell. This will give you a device that works in Turks and Caicos, unlimited calls, texts, and internet. You can rent a phone or a hotspot online before you fly, at the airport or at your hotel when you arrive.

Internet

You can reach the internet in Turks and Caicos via Wi-Fi or cell data. Turks and Caicos have a fast and stable internet link, with speeds of up to 600 Mbps. The islands are linked to the internet via a single underwater fiber-optic line (Arcos-1), which connects the US and several Caribbean countries.

You can find free Wi-Fi in most hotels, houses, restaurants, cafes, bars, and public places on the islands. However, some locations may need more speed or require a password or registration. You can also use Wi-Fi hotspots offered by Flow or Digicel, which are available in some places. You must buy a prepaid ticket or plan to use these sites.

You can use mobile internet on your phone or hotspot if you have a local SIM card or an international plan. Flow and Digicel give 4G service on most islands, but some remote places may only have 2G or 3G coverage. Both services have yet to offer 5G. You can buy prepaid internet deals for your SIM card at different places.

Communication Tips

Turks and Caicos is an easy and handy location for contact and internet connection. Here are some tips to make your conversation easier and more enjoyable:

- The country code for Turks and Caicos is +1 (649). To call a local number from abroad, dial +1 (649) and the seven-digit number. To contact an overseas number from Turks and Caicos, dial + followed by the country code and the number.

- The time zone for Turks and Caicos is UTC-4 (Eastern Standard Time). The islands do not follow daylight saving time.

- The top-level domain (TLD) for Turks and Caicos is .tc. You can find useful information about the islands on websites with this name.

- The official language of Turks and Caicos is English, but you may also hear Creole or other languages spoken by the locals or the newcomers. You can talk easily with anyone on the islands in English, but you may also want to learn some Creole sentences or words to surprise them.

- Be nice and thoughtful when speaking with the locals or the tourists. Use "please", "thank you", "excuse me", and "sorry" when suitable. Be aware of societal differences and try to be open-minded and interested.

Summary

Turks and Caicos is a modern and linked place where you can quickly interact and access the internet. The islands have a stable and fast internet network with two local providers: Flow and Digicel. You can use your phone, buy a local SIM
card, or rent a phone or hotspot. You can also find free Wi-Fi in many places or use cellphone internet. You can speak English easily with anyone on the islands, but you may also hear Creole or other languages spoken by locals or newcomers.

Useful Apps and Websites for Turks and Caicos

Turks and Caicos is a beautiful location that offers many sights and activities for tourists. However, planning your trip can be easier and more fun if you have some useful apps and websites to help you. Here are some of the useful apps and

websites for Turks and Caicos that you should check out before and during your trip.

Visit the Turks and Caicos Islands

Visit the Turks and Caicos Islands is the main tourist website of the country, and it offers detailed and up-to-date information on everything you need to know about the islands. You can find information on entrance requirements, health, safety, customs, transportation, lodging, eating, activities, events, maps, and more. You can also look through pictures, movies, articles, and tips to get motivated and learn more about the culture and past of Turks and Caicos. Visit Turks and Caicos Islands is a trusted and user-friendly website that can help you plan your trip.

Website: https://www.visittci.com/

Weather Underground

Weather Underground is a free app and website that gives accurate and thorough weather predictions for Turks and Caicos. You can see the present conditions, hourly predictions, 10-day forecasts, weather, satellite alerts, and more. You can also modify your settings, apps, and alerts. Weather Underground is a useful app and website for tourists who want to stay updated on the weather conditions in Turks and Caicos.

App Store: https://apps.apple.com/us/app/weather-underground/id486154808

Website: https://www.wunderground.com/

Google Maps

Google Maps is a free app and website that offers maps, routes, navigation, traffic, transit, and more for Turks and Caicos. You can look for places, companies, sites, and more on the map and see pictures, reviews, scores, and contact information. You can also get directions by car, bike, walk, or public transportation and see real-time traffic and travel details. You can also download offline maps, save your favorite places, share your location, and explore nearby areas. Google Maps is a useful app and website for tourists who want to get around Turks and Caicos quickly and efficiently.

App Store: https://apps.apple.com/us/app/google-maps-transit-food/id585027354

Website: https://www.google.com/maps/

You should check out These useful apps and websites for Turks and Caicos before and during your trip. They can help you find the best deals, plan your schedule, learn about the islands, and enjoy your holiday. However, you may also want to explore other apps and websites that fit your unique needs and tastes.

CONCLUSION

Turks and Caicos is a destination that has it all: stunning beaches, turquoise waters, diverse marine life, rich history, lively culture, and delicious food. Whether you want to relax, explore, or learn, you'll find plenty of choices to fit your hobbies and tastes. You can enjoy the islands' natural beauty and wildlife, the people's history and tradition, and the food's tastes and spices. You can also experience the excitement and fun of the activities, the charm and kindness of the locals, and the luxury and comfort of the accommodations. Turks and Caicos is a location that will leave you with long memories and images.

This travel book shows you how to plan your trip to Turks and Caicos, covering the best of what the islands offer. We have given you tips on when to go, where to stay, what to do, what to eat, and what to avoid. We have also provided you with a 7-day schedule to help you maximize your time in Turks and Caicos. We hope this travel guide has motivated you to visit this amazing place and find its wonders.

Turks and Caicos is a location that will beat your hopes and please your senses. It is a location that will make you fall in love with the Caribbean. It is a place that you will want to return to again and again. Turks and Caicos is a location that awaits you. So what are you waiting for? Book your Turks and Caicos trip today and prepare for an amazing holiday!

Printed in Great Britain
by Amazon

28060053R10109